Performance of Valuation Methods in Financial Transactions

Modern Finance, Management Innovation and Economic Growth Set

coordinated by
Faten Ben Bouheni

Volume 4

Performance of Valuation Methods in Financial Transactions

David Heller

iSTE

WILEY

First published 2021 in Great Britain and the United States by ISTE Ltd and John Wiley & Sons, Inc.

ISTE Ltd
27-37 St George's Road
London SW19 4EU
UK

www.iste.co.uk

John Wiley & Sons, Inc.
111 River Street
Hoboken, NJ 07030
USA

www.wiley.com

Library of Congress Control Number: 2020951018

British Library Cataloguing-in-Publication Data
A CIP record for this book is available from the British Library
ISBN 978-1-78630-636-4

Contents

Introduction

In France, public tender offers, public exchange offers and combined offers are all processes of acquisition. The governing regulations of the *Autorité des marchés financiers* (AMF) guide how these public offers are carried out. Before they are launched, the initiator, with the help of their advisory bank, undertakes a process of analysis, with the main objective of determining the financial capacity of the business, in order to reach an offer price that will be proposed to the security holders of the company under evaluation. As underlined by Bellalah (1998), the shareholder will only divest their shares to the initiator of the offer if they consider the price proposed to be satisfactory. Therefore, the market capitalization of the target company is not enough to constitute the benchmark for the offer price; the evaluation must always follow an approach informed by multiple criteria.

The direct link between the profit reaped from a company's investments and the profit demanded by the company's investors will determine the quality of the investment policy pursued. By generating cash flows such that they maximize the amount of value created by the economic asset, a well-conducted investment policy will result in a higher return on investment than that demanded by investors. The economic value of shareholder equity will then increase. However, if the investment policy fails, the shareholder may sanction the company in question by selling its securities. They will then face financial difficulties, insofar as their economic assets have been devalued. And so, the shareholder has the power to grant funds to the company, and must, in this scenario, understand how to properly evaluate the company's assets from an economic perspective, as well as their shareholder equity.

Beyond a sufficiently profitable investment policy, maximizing the value of economic assets comes from an optimal financial structure. Indeed, in order to determine the value of the economic asset, the cash flows that result from the investment policy are brought in line with the cost of capital. In this instance, it would be possible to have the ability to maximize this rate by using an appropriate financial policy. Evaluation regarding the structure of liabilities must include considerations that go well beyond the simple cost of different sources of financial gain. There are three major elements to take into account when looking to evaluate the feasibility of an optimal financial policy: these are taxation, both at the level of the company and of the individual, consideration of the costs of dysfunction and bankruptcy that an additional amount of debt would incur, and the behavioral phenomena in theories created by organizations. Indeed, beyond the framework of the theory of market equilibrium which considers the company to be a single player, conflicts between the various stakeholders, who do not always share the same interests nor make the same choices when it comes to the correct financial policy to be adopted, inevitably impact the nature and distribution of the funds that are granted to the company.

The traditional valuation of equity can be undertaken indirectly by first estimating the economic asset, and then subtracting the value of net debt after adjustment, or directly by adopting an average industry multiple. Within the acquisition market and in view of the sums involved, the valuation of the target company is essential to be able to come to a target buyback price for which a control premium is calculated, and before embarking on any negotiations with potential buyers. In short, valuation helps to make decisions about an opportunity for merger or partnership. More generally, this exercise is designed to help position the company within its particular market in terms of performance, as well as to improve the way it is managed and run, with a view to generate value by working on the areas that have been identified as weaknesses. In addition to this, valuation constitutes a tool that facilitates the development of a company that is seeking out opportunities for new financial support and entering new markets, for example. Finally, valuing the securities of the company allows us to comply with tax legislation and potentially reap the rewards that it offers.

The target price of a company can be fixed according to its assets, its competitors or even how it is predicted to progress into the future. A business plan will encompass all of these aspects. In practice, business valuation is carried out by at least three types of professionals: Financial analysts, who determine target prices for listed companies and provide recommendations on whether to buy, sell or hold stock. Corporate and investment banks assess companies for mergers and acquisitions. In France, if the target company is listed, its valuation must be submitted to the AMF in order to justify that the offer price is satisfactory for all of the stakeholders involved. The evaluation is therefore incorporated into a specific document that is sent to the organization with the aim of obtaining a visa. Here, several valuation methods may come into play. The offer price is the result of an analysis informed by multiple criteria. If the company is not listed, a public offer for tender is usually initiated by the banks. In this case, the seller's advisory bank sends a document that briefly describes the characteristics of the company to be sold to potential buyers. Questioned at the start about their possible interest in the company, the potential buyers formulate an indicative offer based on their own valuation of the target company and an informative note which contains past accounts and the business plan. Then, potential acquirers may put forward a binding offer, which may be significantly different from that conceived at the beginning, on the basis of receiving additional data from due diligence services following meetings with management. Corporate and investment banks also perform equity capital market valuations during initial public offerings, and more traditional issuances. Finally, the transactions, for which the private equity analysts are responsible, are carried out with leverage buy out (LBO). Their approach is different, as the value of the target company is a result of the resources (equity and debts) that can be raised by a holding company that is created *ad hoc*. Capital investors demand an internal rate of return of 20% over 3–5 years. The debt raised from banks has its own constraints: 80% of senior debt is absorbed on a linear basis over 7 years, and 20% is reimbursed in the end.

Professionals and academics believe that there are three main categories of methods that must be combined to carry out an evaluation of a company and its equity. The comparables method is based on evaluation via sector multiples from listed companies or via transaction multiples. The discounted cash flows approach deems the value of a company to be the sum of its future cash flows, discounted using the weighted average cost of capital. Cash flows are calculated using the operating income, and the discount rate includes, on the one hand, the cost of equity derived from the capital asset pricing model and, on the other hand, the cost of debt. Finally, asset-based methods are based on the sum of the parts that represent the sum of assets.

This method is used in particular by value holding companies and conglomerates for integrating unrealized capital gains and losses restated for hypothetical elements. For listed companies, market capitalization provides a fourth value, which cannot be ignored, regardless of the size of the floating business. When the valuation is undertaken in order to merge a target company with the company at the origin of the offer, the process is able to be undertaken, provided that funds can be raised to carry out the process and that the benefit of the initiator's action is fully assessed in relation to the synergies that are envisaged from the merger.

In this context, it seems interesting to ponder over traditional valuation methods. In what circumstances are they relevant and reliable and, according to specific situations, to what extent is it more appropriate to favor certain methods over others? The term "relevant" justifies why various methods must be evaluated, as they aim to demonstrate equality when coming to the final value of a company.

Chapter 1 aims to bring to light a theoretical framework regarding the possibility of optimizing the financial structure, the various methods of traditional valuations and the possibilities of applying them within the acquisition market, such as the structuring of financial arrangements with the leverage effect. Chapter 2 is dedicated to a study of the financial literature that highlights the theoretical adjustments that can be made to improve the performance of these methods, how they are used according to specific empirical contexts and how value is created as a result of company mergers.

1

Traditional Valuation Methods and Ways of Applying Them

1.1. Introduction

It is imperative that the investments of a business generate a sufficient level of profitability to satisfy the demands held by the investors. If the obtained (or predicted) level of profitability is higher than the level of profitability that is expected given the risk, the value of the economic asset increases, impacting the value of shares in an upward fashion[1]. Otherwise, the investor will not be satisfied with the profitability of their investment in relation to the risk absorbed to sell their security. Enterprise and share value thus will fluctuate in a downwards fashion. And so, the direct consequence of the investment policy is a variation in economic value of equity, i.e. the market capitalization if the company is listed[2]. It thus follows that an investor's power lies, on the one hand, in their decision to allocate funds to the company (without financial backing, the company is no more) and, on the other hand, in the evaluation of the economic asset through securities that have already been issued[3]. Consequently, changes in the value of economic assets are reflected almost entirely on market capitalization. When the company faces significant difficulties, the role of creditors changes because

1 Enterprise value is equal to the economic value of equity and net debt. However, as long as the company is in a normal situation, the value of debts will fluctuate mainly according to the level of interest rates.

2 This rule can be applied sooner or later to companies that are not listed upon sale, merger, succession or increase in capital.

3 Market capitalization represents the economic value of equity and net debt, which represent a decreased value of loans granted by creditors for cash investments.

from a financial perspective, they then own the company. When the equity value is almost zero, adjustments can only be made through the net debt, whose value becomes lower than the nominal value. Therefore, liabilities are the screen placed between the value of economic assets and the financial decisions taken by investors.

Just as the investment policy is able to create or destroy value, the financial policy through the financial structure can theoretically change the value of equity. It is not so much of question of increasing the free cash flow of economic assets as it is of reducing the weighted average cost of capital, synonymous with the financial cost of the company, i.e. the minimum rate of return that assets must generate. In this way, it seems pertinent to interrogate whether an optimal liability structure can be created. The said structure would enable the cost of capital to be minimized, thereby maximizing the enterprise value.

To guide their decisions to allocate their resources to companies, investors use traditional valuation methods. In this way, the economic valuation of shareholder equity can be obtained by relying on a stock market analysis by comparing the aggregate multiples of the balance sheet and/or the income statement, or by undertaking a transactional comparison of the processes being carried out in the sector that the company to be valued operates in. Furthermore, by producing a business plan, i.e. by providing free cash flows that are discounted at the cost of capital, the investors may estimate the value of the company based on its future plans. Finally, by adopting a proprietary approach, investors are able to concentrate on the real assets held at a given time by the company. These three approaches are in theory supposed to be combined in order to refine the valuation further. With this in mind, it becomes ever more important to investigate whether an optimal capital structure really exists. Indeed, when it comes to carrying out a valuation by discounting free cash flows, two possibilities arise in terms of maximizing the enterprise value. Either the investment policy is relevant in itself, as it generates significant cash flows which lie in the numerator of the formula, or it is possible to consider that an adequate financial policy is carried out on condition that it decreases the cost of capital, which is at the denominator of the formula. In both of these scenarios, the enterprise value is increased.

Auditing activities come in particular from this type of valuation exercise. Theories from organizations, which help to explain the levels of corporate debts, go beyond outlining how to adopt acquisition strategies. Indeed, the very nature of shareholding encourages one to implement different types of financial arrangement that influence both the evolution of the power of holders of capital and the choice of which financial structure to adopt in order to acquire the target company.

1.2. The cost of financial structure

The portfolio theory from Markovitz (1959) deals with determining the cost of equity. The investor's profitability demand depends on their degree of risk aversion. The portfolio to be chosen is graphically located at the intersection of the efficient frontier and one of the curves that characterizes the investor's iso-utility. Sharpe (1963) simplifies this theory by assuming that the expected return on an asset is linked to the return on a market index. Thus, the investor's demand for profitability depends solely on systematic risk. Efficient diversification of an asset portfolio eliminates the specific risk of the share.

An economic reading of a balance sheet consists of identifying, at a given moment, all the jobs involved in the company's operating cycle and the origin of its resources. Economic assets (or enterprise value) are the sum of fixed assets and working capital requirements, i.e. all of the network in progress that is aligned with the operating and investment cycle[4]. Economic assets are financed by equity and net debt. And so, the market value of the economic asset is divided between the market value of these two types of resources. This results in a balance sheet of the company that only includes market values. In this context, the question arises as to whether there is an optimal capital structure that maximizes enterprise value and thereby minimizes the cost of capital.

The traditional approach, wherein evaluation is carried out without taxation, ensures that there is an optimal liability structure resulting from a sound use of the leverage effect. By also considering a tax-free approach, equilibrium market theory asserts, on the contrary, that there is no optimal capital structure because investors are able to duplicate at their level the financial operations of companies without cost and without any additional risk. The arbitrations that they can mobilize in the event of initial situations

4 We may also call this "operational asset" or "capital employed".

where the financial structures would be different lead to a rebalancing of the market. That is to say, they help to ensure that the value of the financial liabilities of two companies that are equal in every aspect becomes equal again. In the presence of taxation, the value of an indebted company is equal to that of a company that is not indebted, to which we must add to the present value of the tax savings linked to the tax deductibility of interest charges. However, even in the presence of taxation, the theories presented by organizations teach us that the choice of whether or not to go into debt comes more from the agent conflicts between the different parties such as shareholders and creditors, or from signals sent to the market more than from intrinsic costs.

1.2.1. *Financial asset valuation*

The models for valuating financial assets or the capital assets pricing model (CAPM) is used to evaluate the equity of a company in a balanced market. This formula provides an estimate of the rate of return expected by the market for a financial asset according to its systematic risk.

Markowitz (1959) states that between two portfolios characterized by their supposedly random return, one would retain, at identical risk, the company with the highest expected return and, with the same expected return, the company with the lower risk. This principle means that a number of portfolios may be dismissed, as they are less efficient than others. The efficient frontier represents the curve that connects the set of efficient portfolios. The portfolios that sit below this curve are rejected.

Consequently, it is possible to determine the weight of two assets that appear in a portfolio in order to minimize the risk thereof:

$$R_p = x_A R_A + x_B R_B \quad [1.1]$$

$$R_p = x_A R_A + (1 - x_A) R_B \quad [1.2]$$

$$V(R_p) = x_A^2 V(R_A) + (1 - x_A)^2 V(R_B) + 2x_A(1 - x_A)\mathrm{cov}(R_A, R_B) \quad [1.3]$$

$$V(R_p) = x_A^2 V(R_A) + V(R_B) - 2x_A V(R_B) + x_A^2 V(R_B)$$
$$+2x_A \mathrm{cov}(R_A, R_B) - 2x_A^2 \mathrm{cov}(R_A, R_B) \quad [1.4]$$

or:

– R_p: portfolio return;

– x_i: weight of asset *i* in the portfolio.

Variance is minimal when its derivative is zero. We then look for x_A such that:

$$\frac{dV(R_p)}{dx_A} = V'[R_p] = 0 \quad [1.5]$$

As a result:

$$V'(R_p) = 2x_A - 2.V(R_A) + 2x_A V(R_B) + 2cov(R_A, R_B) - 4x_A cov(R_A, R_B) = 0 \quad [1.6]$$

$$V'(R_p) = x_A - V(R_A) + x_A V(R_B) + cov(R_A, R_B) - 2x_A cov(R_A, R_B) = 0 \quad [1.7]$$

$$x_A = \frac{V(R_B) - cov(R_A, R_B)}{V(R_A) + V(R_B) - 2.cov(R_A, R_B)} \quad [1.8]$$

Now considering R_p, the portfolio return made up of *n* assets characterized by their respective return $R_1, \ldots, R_n$, we have:

$$R_p = \frac{1}{n}\sum_{i=1}^{n} R_i \quad [1.9]$$

In order to determine $E(R_p)$ and $V(R_p)$, we suppose that:

$$E(R_1) = E(R_2) = \ldots = E(R_n) = E \quad [1.10]$$

$$V(R_1) = V(R_2) = \ldots = V(R_n) = \sigma^2 \quad [1.11]$$

$$E(R_p) = E\left(\frac{1}{n}\sum_{i=1}^{n} R_i\right) = \frac{1}{n}\sum_{i=1}^{n} E(R_i) = \frac{1}{n}\sum_{i=1}^{n} E = E \quad [1.12]$$

Assume first that the returns of each of the *n* assets fluctuate independently of each other. In this case, the variance of a sum is equal to the sum of its variances. And so:

$$V(R_p) = V\left(\frac{1}{n}\sum_{i=1}^{n} R_i\right) = \frac{1}{n^2}\sum_{i=1}^{n} V(R_i) = \frac{1}{n^2}\sum_{i=1}^{n} \sigma^2 = \frac{\sigma^2}{n} \quad [1.13]$$

If n approaches infinity, then $\frac{\sigma^2}{n}$ goes to 0.

We then suppose that the performance of each of the n assets is correlated with each other. In this case:

$$V(R_p) = V\left(\frac{1}{n}\sum_{i=1}^{n} R_i\right) = \frac{1}{n^2}\sum_{i=1}^{n} V(R_i) + \frac{2}{n^2}\sum_{1\leq i\leq j\leq n} \operatorname{cov}(R_i, R_j)$$
$$= \frac{\sigma^2}{n} + \frac{2}{n^2}S \tag{1.14}$$

where:

$$S = \sum_{1\leq i<j\leq n} \operatorname{cov}(R_i, R_j)$$

Let $\bar{C}$ be the average covariance of portfolio P. By definition:

$$\bar{C} = \frac{\sum_{1\leq i<j\leq n} \operatorname{cov}(R_i, R_j)}{N} = \frac{S}{N} \tag{1.15}$$

where N corresponds to the number of covariances.

In total, the number N of terms is equal to 0 + 1 + … + (n – 1), so:

$$\sum_{i=1}^{n-1} i = \frac{n(n-1)}{2} \tag{1.16}$$

Like:

$$\bar{C} = \frac{S}{N} \tag{1.17}$$

One has:

$$S = N.\bar{C} \tag{1.18}$$

Consequently:

$$V(R_p) = \frac{\sigma^2}{n} + \frac{2}{n^2}S = \frac{\sigma^2}{n} + \frac{2}{n^2}\frac{n(n-1)}{2}\bar{C} = \frac{\sigma^2}{n} + \frac{n(n-1)}{n^2}\bar{C} \tag{1.19}$$

When n approaches infinity, $\frac{\sigma^2}{n}$ approaches 0 and $\frac{n(n-1)}{n^2}$ approaches the ratio of terms of higher degree. This ratio is equal to 1. By multiplying this result by $\bar{C}$, we may deduce that $V(R_p)$ approaches the mean covariance $\bar{C}$. The risk equal to the standard deviation of R_p cannot therefore be eliminated, even by diversifying the portfolio insofar as it therefore approaches the square root of the mean covariance.

On the graph, this means that the curve that represents the risk as a function of the number of securities that are contained within the portfolio admits a horizontal asymptote of equation $y = \bar{C}$.

The basis of the CAPM comes from the hypothesis within the Markowitz model, i.e. a portfolio for which performance R_p is defined as:

$$R_p = \sum_{i=1}^{n} X_i R_i \qquad [1.20]$$

We assume moreover that the performance R_i of each asset *i* is linearly related to a market index denoted I. In other words, $R_i = \alpha_i + \beta_i I + \varepsilon_i$, where I and ε_i are a random variable that presents the following properties:

– $E(\varepsilon_i) = 0$;

– $V(\varepsilon_i) = \text{constant}$;

– $\text{Cov}(\varepsilon_i \varepsilon_j) = 0$ for 2 assets *i* and *j* becoming part of the portfolio.

In this case, the choice of portfolio located on the efficient frontier which should be retained according to the degree of the investor's risk aversion is simpler. It comes from solving a system of equations that correspond to the inversion of an almost diagonal matrix (it is then necessary to consider the inverses of the numbers located on the diagonal). The financial asset equilibrium model, from which the formula for the capital market line (used to determine the cost of equity) is derived, makes the simplified hypothesis model from Sharpe (1963) endogenous. In other words, this method consists of replacing the index I from the Sharpe formula with the performance R_M of the whole market.

The formula is thus:

$$R_i = \alpha_i + \beta_i R_M + \varepsilon_i \qquad [1.21]$$

When looking at a portfolio P composed of *n* assets *i* each of them entering for a proportion X_i, the portfolio yield is as follows:

$$R_p = \sum_{i=1}^{n} X_i R_i \qquad [1.22]$$

We can thus calculate:

$$cov(R_p, R_M) = cov(\sum_{i=1}^{n} X_i R_i, R_M) = \sum_{i=1}^{n} X_i cov(R_i, R_M) \qquad [1.23]$$

And then:

$$\beta_p = \frac{cov(R_p, R_M)}{V(R_M)} = \sum_{i=1}^{n} \frac{X_i cov(R_i, R_M)}{V(R_M)} \qquad [1.24]$$

$$\beta_p = X_1\beta_1 + X_2\beta_2 + \cdots + X_n\beta_n = \sum_{i=1}^{n} X_i\beta_i \qquad [1.25]$$

As a result, the beta of a portfolio is the weighted average of the betas of the assets that make it up.

Let us consider a portfolio composed of a market index contract and non-risky securities. For example:

– X_M: proportion of market index contracts in the portfolio;

– β_M: beta of market index contracts;

– β_F: beta of non-risky securities;

– R_F: risk-free rate.

Based on the weighted beta formula, the beta for this portfolio is:

$$\beta_p = X_M\beta_M + (1 - X_M)\beta_F \qquad [1.26]$$

As β_M is the beta of market index contracts, $\beta_M = 1$.

And β_F is the beta of non-risky securities, $\beta_F = 0$.

So:

$$\beta_p = X_M.1 + (1 - X_M)0 \text{ or } X_M = \beta_p \qquad [1.27]$$

Since:

$$R_p = X_M R_M + (1 - X_M) R_F \quad [1.28]$$

We can deduce that:

$$R_p = \beta_p R_M + (1 - \beta_M) R_F = R_F + \beta_p (R_M - R_F) \quad [1.29]$$

By setting p = I, i.e. a portfolio reduced to asset *i*:

$$R_i = R_F + \beta_i (R_M - R_F) \quad [1.30]$$

where:

– R_i: share return *i*;

– R_m: market yield;

– β_i: systematic risk of company share *i*;

– R_f: risk-free rate;

– $R_m - R_f$: market risk premium.

Systematic asset risk represents the coefficient of volatility of the stock, relative to the market. If β_i is greater than 1, the share is said to be aggressive and the variations in market yield are increased at the level of the return of the share. If β_i is less than 1, the share is said to be defensive and the variations in market yield are reduced at the share level. Finally, if β_i is equal to 1, the share replicates the market.

The weighted average cost of capital (WACC), denoted K, is the average annual rate of return that a company's assets must generate. It is the minimum rate required by the shareholders and creditors of the company to agree to finance its investments and projects. K is the weighted average of equity and net debt. The weighting is a function of their weight within the value of the economic asset. To be noted:

– k_D: rate of return required by creditors after tax;

– k_{CP}: rate of return required by shareholders (previously, R_i);

– V_D: market value of net debt;

– V_{CP}: market value of equity

$$K = k_{CP} \frac{V_{CP}}{V_{CP}+V_D} + k_D \frac{V_D}{V_{CP}+V_D} \quad [1.31]$$

Economic assets are financed by equity and net debt. Market value is split between that of net debt and that of equity. The question then is where there is an optimal capital structure that minimizes the cost of capital. In other words, it seems evident that the enterprise value increases with a sound investment policy because it generates, in this case, significant cash flow. What is more, since the balance sheet is in equilibrium, can we say that it is reasonable to consider that an optimal financial policy (one that results from a perfect distribution between equity and debt) can maximize this same enterprise value, due to minimizing the cost of capital?

1.2.2. *Optimal capital structure*

According to the traditional approach, in the absence of taxation, both for the company (absence of corporate tax) and for the investor (absence of income tax and capital gains tax), there is an optimal liability structure that maximizes the value of the economic asset and therefore minimizes the cost of capital through the measured use of debt and its leverage effect.

The company value is a product of discounting the cash flow that is available at rate K. Since debt is less risky, it is less expensive than equity. Thus, any moderate increase in debt decreases the WACC to the extent that a cheaper resource (debt) is substituted for a more expensive resource (equity). Having said this, any increase in debt in the weight of financing increases the risk of the shareholder passing it on to the cost of equity, which will cancel part of the decrease in total financial cost. In addition, at a certain level of debt owed, the cost also increases due to the increase of risk. The operation can be repeated until the requirement for the rate of return on equity is so high that it cancels out the positive effect of additional debt. At this level of financial leverage, the company has reached its optimal capital structure, as it has the lowest possible WACC (or cost of funding) and therefore the highest economic asset value.

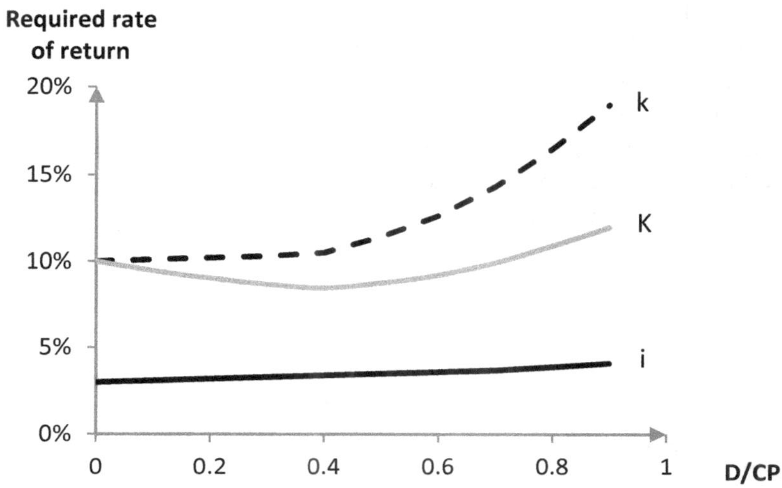

Figure 1.1. *Optimal weighted average cost of capital according to the traditional approach*

According to the theory of market equilibrium, in the absence of taxation, the enterprise value of two identical companies with different financial structures is the same. This is because investors can reproduce financial transactions at their level without additional cost and risk. In other words, when undertaking a valuation of the company, they are indifferent to any financial construction. Modigliani and Miller (1958) affirm that arbitrations made by investors imply that there cannot be an ideal liability structure in a market that is in equilibrium.

When *i* increases, the rhythm at which *k* progresses will slow down, such that K remains constant: stakeholders are relieved of part of the risk of the company that is passed on to the creditors as soon as the amount of debt becomes significant. In a market in equilibrium, the increase in expected profitability linked to the leverage effect and the increase in risk offset each other so that the value of the share remains the same. The increase in the level of debt that a company has increases the risk of the shareholder as well as the profitability that they require. This is so that ultimately the wealth of shareholders does not change. The value of debt comes down to the exact price that has to be paid for equity. In other words, one should not pay the company twice by buying the shares at the cost of the economic asset and then paying off the debts. Asset value is the same whether it is financed by debt, equity or both. The weighted average cost of capital of the company is independent of its two sources of financing. Debt and equity will adjust according to any change in financial structure. Indeed, increasing debt does not make the cost of capital decrease. On the contrary, debt increases the risk for shareholders and therefore the rate of return that they demand. The weighted average cost of capital is constant regardless of the financial structure.

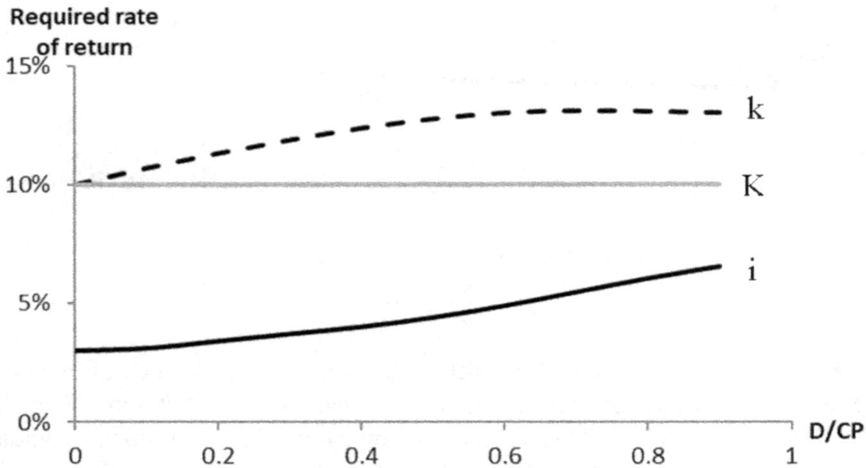

Figure 1.2. *Modern theory of financial structure*

From a mathematical perspective, the cost of capital of a company (independent of its financial structure) corresponds with the capitalization rate ρ of the expected operating profit of a company without debt and belonging to the same industrial risk class[5]. In other words, this leads us to consider that the enterprise value is akin to a perpetual growth rate of constant future operating results discounted at the rate ρ:

$$VE = \sum_{t=1}^{+\infty} \frac{E(REX)}{(1+\rho)^t} = \frac{E(REX)}{\rho} \qquad [1.32]$$

5 In practice, from the same sector of activity.

The cost of equity *k* corresponds to the financial profitability r_f insofar as we can reason it *ad infinitum*. From there:

$$k = \rho + (\rho - i)\frac{D}{CP} \quad [1.33]$$

This theory does not explain the everyday reality for two key reasons. On the one hand, by conserving the same market logic, biases start to emerge. They explain why a business goes into debt and why it does not go beyond a certain threshold. The fundamental parameters are taxation and the costs of bankruptcy associated with excessive debt. On the other hand, there are interferences between the financial structure and the investment which can be explained above all by the divergent interests of different financial partners in terms of value creation and by the divergent personal situations in terms of access to certain information.

Modigliani and Miller (1963) perfected their theory by taking into account corporate tax. When we consider corporate tax, the result is that debt is favored over equity. In fact, financial expenses are deductible from the tax base on companies. The company's creditors collect them without having already been taxed. However, dividends are not deductible. The shareholders receive them after tax payment. In a sense, deducted financial expenses can be seen as a state subsidy to the indebted company. So that they can benefit, it is enough for the expenses to be taxable, i.e. it is a beneficiary. If the company uses debt on a permanent basis, it will benefit from a tax economy that is considered at the level of the value of its economic asset:

$$X^* = EBIT\,(1 - \tau) \quad [1.34]$$

$$X = (EBIT - iV_D)\,(1 - \tau) + iV_D = EBIT\,(1 - t) + iV_D\tau \quad [1.35]$$

$$X = X^* + iV_D\tau \quad [1.36]$$

where:

– X: renumeration of capital providers to the indebted company;

– X*: renumeration of capital providers to the company without debt;

– VE: value of the assets of an indebted company;

– VE*: value of the assets of a company without debt;

– *i*: cost of debt;

– ρ: cost of the capital of a company without debt;

– V_D: market value of debt;

– V_{CP}: market value of equity;

– EBIT: operating result;

– τ: corporate tax rate;

– iV_D: financial expenses;

– $iV_D\tau$: tax reduction generated by the deductibility of financial expenses;

– shareholders receive all of the corporate profits.

If we consider that the value of the assets corresponds to a perpetual annuity of future flows, then the flows of the company with no debt are discounted at the rate ρ, i.e. $VE^* = \frac{X^*}{\rho}$ and the tax reduction if discounted at the cost of debt. Moreover:

$$VE = \frac{X^*}{\rho} + \frac{iV_D\tau}{i} + VE^* + V_D\tau \qquad [1.37]$$

In the case of corporate tax, the value of the economic assets of a company with debt is equal to the value of the economic assets of a company without debt, increased by the present value of the related tax savings. This saving will only be effective if the profitability of the company is sufficient and it does not benefit from other exemptions (tax loss carryforwards, research tax credit, etc.). This is the basis of the APV method (adjusted present value), which separately recommends valuing economic assets by discounting cash flow and the value of the tax savings generated by financial expenses. The question then is to know the discount rate of the tax savings due to the tax deductibility of financial expenses. Modigliani and Miller advocate discounting the tax savings to the cost of debt.

This method is appropriate if one thinks that these tax savings are certain. Therefore, the value of the tax savings is equal to the value of the debt multiplied by the tax rate. On the other hand, it is commendable to think that the company will not be forever in debt, being the receiving party and taxed at the same rate. In this way, it is quite conceivable to discount the tax savings to the cost of equity, especially since it goes to the shareholder.

As a result, the adjusted cost of capital is first obtained by determining the cost of equity:

$$k = \frac{E(RN)}{CP} = \frac{(E(EBIT) - iD)(1 - \tau)}{CP} \qquad [1.38]$$

$$k = \frac{E(EBIT)(1 - \tau)}{CP} - iD\frac{1 - \tau}{CP} \qquad [1.39]$$

Recalling that the enterprise value VE* corresponds to a perpetual annuity of operating results (constant in the future) discounted at ρ or at the enterprise value VE minus the tax savings linked to the debt, we have:

$$k = \rho + (\rho - i)(1 - \tau)\frac{D}{CP} \qquad [1.40]$$

And so, the cost of capital K equals:

$$K = k\frac{CP}{CP+D} + i(1 - \tau)\frac{D}{CP+D} \qquad [1.41]$$

$$K = \rho - \rho\tau\frac{D}{CP+D} \qquad [1.42]$$

$$K = \rho\left[1 - \frac{D\tau}{CP+D}\right] \qquad [1.43]$$

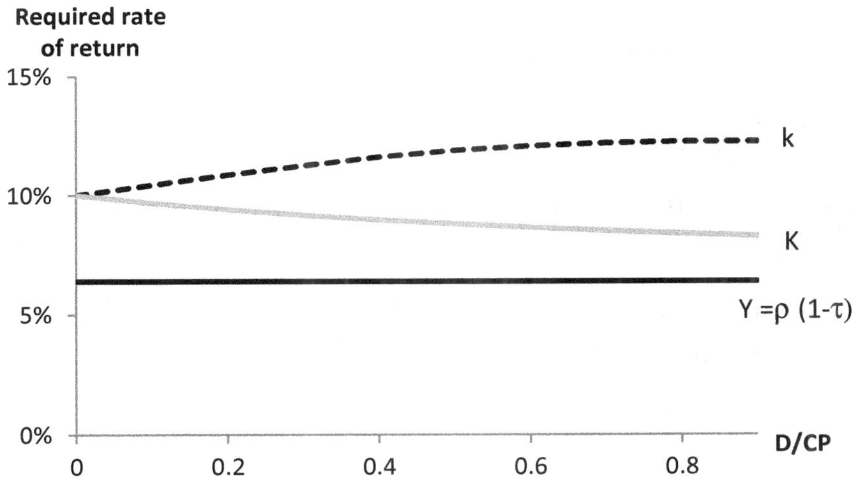

Figure 1.3. *Adjusted cost of capital*

The cost of capital thus is not affected by an increase in the cost of debt because the formula for the adjusted cost of capital does not contain *i*. In addition, Modigliani and Miller's formula for the cost of capital expresses that an increase in the cost of debt *i* leads to a decrease in the cost of equity *k*.

The increase in debt burden in finance can be translated into a fall in the cost of capital. Therefore, the increase in debt burden results in an increase in enterprise value. The difference between the enterprise value of the company in debt and the enterprise value of the company not in debt corresponds to the value of the tax-saving perpetual annuity generated by the tax deductibility of financial expenses. In other words, the increase in debt only has the effect of increasing the value of tax credit (the change in the financial structure, as it has no impact on the value of industrial assets).

Hamada (1972) is influenced by the work of Modigliani and Miller when defining the equation of unlevered beta of a share. Starting from the cost of equity:

$$k = \rho + (\rho - i)(1 - \tau)\frac{D}{CP} \qquad [1.44]$$

The CAPM equation is used, while assuming that the company is in debt at the risk-free rate (in this case $i = r_f$):

$$k = r_f + \beta_i[E(R_M) - r_f] \qquad [1.45]$$

$$\beta_i^* = \frac{\beta_i}{1 + \frac{D(1-\tau)}{CP}} \qquad [1.46]$$

Assuming the firm is in debt above the risk-free rate, CAPM is applied to the debt using the β_D debt beta:

$$r_f + \beta_i[E(R_M) - r_f] = r_f + \beta_i^*[E(R_M) - r_f] + [r_f + \beta_i^*[E(R_M) - r_f]] - r_f - \beta_D[E(R_M) - r_f](1 - \tau)\frac{D}{CP} \qquad [1.47]$$

$$\beta_i = \beta_i^* + \beta_i^* - \beta_D(1 - \tau)\frac{D}{CP} \qquad [1.48]$$

However, the costs of bankruptcy are the first limitation to this reasoning. Indeed, a company that has recurrent debt runs the risk of no longer being able to meet its commitments. If this is the case, the company files for bankruptcy, which theoretically qualifies as a reallocation of assets for productivity purposes. For an investor with a perfectly diversified portfolio, bankruptcy is seen as a mechanism for reallocating resources. The cost is therefore zero. However, in practice, markets do not work perfectly. Bankruptcy has a real cost because of its very nature. The decrease in enterprise value resulting from the inclusion of the costs of bankruptcy has been studied in particular by Molina (2005), Almeida (2007) and Bae (2011). The judicial liquidation of a company generates:

– direct costs: severance pay, attorney fees, legal costs, shareholder efforts to obtain a liquidation bonus, etc.;

– indirect costs: canceled orders (for fear that they won't be honored), reduction in supplier credits (for fear of never being paid back), impact on productivity (strikes), inability to obtain funding, etc.

From this perspective, the bankruptcy of a company can be perceived as the refusal of shareholders to offer additional funds. They consider their previous bets to be lost. Shareholders effectively hand the company over to its creditors who thus become the new stakeholders. Creditors bear the full cost of the company's demise, which further reduces the possibility of debts being paid back. Even though they don't go as far as bankruptcy, the company with great debt faces the costs of dysfunction which penalize its value: a reduction of the cost of research and development, maintenance, training or marketing (in order to meet the debt deadlines), difficulty in finding new resources to finance profitable projects, demotivation of some of the staff members, etc.

Due to tax deductibility, tax can create value. A business with debt may be worth more than a business with no debt. This point cannot be overstated for two main reasons. On the one hand, in times of crisis, excessive debt leads tax advantage to disappear (the company does not make enough profits). On the other hand, it can make dysfunction and bankruptcy costs emerge. The value of a company with debt can thus be broken down as follows:

Value of the company with no debt
+ Present value of the tax savings related to debt
– Present value of bankruptcy and dysfunction costs [1.49]
= Value of the company with debt

The above reasoning can also be broken down in terms of the weighted average cost of capital. That is to say, when the company goes into debt, the cost of capital will be reduced thanks to the tax savings on interest. But when the company approaches bankruptcy, the costs of bankruptcy are factored into the rate of return demanded by investors. Paradoxically, we can uncover the traditional theory which advocates controlled debt. The optimal theoretical debt ratio is achieved when the present value of the tax savings due to additional debt is just offset by the increase in the present value of bankruptcy and dysfunction costs.

Investor taxation is the second limit to the reasoning. Miller (1977) echoes the 1958 conclusions from Modigliani concerning the lack of an optimal financial structure. In his theory, taxation is taken into account both at the level of the company and at the level of the investor. Miller argues that the effect of income tax cancels out that of corporate taxes so that the value of an economic asset is the same, regardless of the liability structure that finances it. The author observes that in general, investors are taxed more personally on debt income than on equity income. In other words, the tax advantage of debt at the corporate level is thwarted by the tax advantage of equity at the investor level. There is therefore no one source of funding that prevails over another:

$$X^* = EBIT\,(1 - t_s)\,(1 - t_a)$$

and:

$$X = (EBIT - iV_D)\,(1 - t_s)\,(1 - t_a) + iV_D\,(1 - t_o) \qquad [1.50]$$

and:

$$X = X^* + iV_D(1 - t_0)\left[1 - \frac{(1-t_s)(1-t_a)}{(1-t_0)}\right] \qquad [1.51]$$

where:

– r_f: risk-free rate;

– t_s: corporate tax rate;

– t_a: tax rate (legal persons) on the remuneration of shares;

– t_o: tax rate (legal persons) on the renumeration of bonds.

The value of assets corresponds to a perpetual annuity of future cash flows. Therefore, the flows of the company without debt are discounted at the rate ρ and the flows generated by the debt are discounted at the risk-free rate r_f. So:

$$V = \frac{X^*}{\rho} + \frac{iV_D(1-t_o)}{r_f}\left[1 - \frac{(1-t_s)(1-t_a)}{(1-t_o)}\right] \quad [1.52]$$

$$V = V^* + \frac{iV_D(1-t_o)}{r_f}\left[1 - \frac{(1-t_s)(1-t_a)}{(1-t_o)}\right] \quad [1.53]$$

Let V_D' be the capitalized value of debt for lenders:

$$V_D' = \frac{iV_D(1-t_o)}{r_f} \quad [1.54]$$

And let G′ be the possible gain due to debt:

$$G' = V_D'\left[1 - \frac{(1-t_s)(1-t_a)}{1-t_o}\right] \quad [1.55]$$

Therefore, if $(1-t_o) = (1-t_s)(1-t_a)$, then $G' = 0$.

Factoring in investor income tax can reduce the debt benefit. Ultimately, it should be kept in mind that from this set of controversies, taxation is an essential parameter in absolute terms, but that it is unlikely that it serves to fully explain the financial structure of companies. What is more, the cost of debt *per se* may not be sufficient to explain a business's choice as to whether or not to take out a loan. Indeed, the theory of markets in equilibrium starts from the affirmation that the company is a single player. Therefore, it ignores any conflicts that may arise between different stakeholders within the company as they may pursue different or even opposing goals. In this context, taking out debt can be seen more as a signal, beyond the financial considerations that are implied.

1.2.3. *Theories of organizations*

Signaling theory maintains that company executives have more information than funders and are better able to forecast future cash flows of the business. Thus, any signal emitted to show that flows are better than expected or that the risk is lower than expected enables the creation of value for the investor. In order for the signal to be credible, it must have its own sanction if it is proved to be wrong. Debt is seen as an indicator of the good health of a company since the manager of an underperforming company cannot go into debt. It reflects the manager's desire to improve the financial performance of their company in order to generate the cash flows necessary to service the new debt. Synonymous with a market that bears good news, the loan generates a rise in stock prices. Ross (1977), Blazenko (1987), John (1987) and Narayanan (1988) have notably studied the role of debt as a signal given to the market on the financial health of companies. Indeed, the managers of a company whose debt is increasing signal to the market that they know the company's status, that it is favorable and that the performance of the company will by consequence allow them to pay additional financial charges and repay this new debt without difficulty. And so, perhaps a signal does not tell us about the financial structure of a company, but rather its ability to transform. On the other hand, announcing an increase in capital leads to a drop in the share price. Indeed, directors do not carry out capital increases when the value appears to them to be undervalued (so as to not place their current shareholders in an unfavorable situation). If there is an unjustified increase in capital, the investor will deduce that the stock price is overvalued and that is why the current shareholders accept the emergence of shares. It is therefore evident that if a director sells their stake in a company, it is a negative signal. This means that they have internal information; that the value of future cash flows, taking into account the risk, is lower than the price at which they can negotiate their participation in the company. Conversely, any strengthening of their participation in the company, especially if it is financed by debt, will be a very positive signal for the market.

The preference theory or pecking order theory, initially presented by Myers and Majluf (1984), justifies the prioritization of funding methods. It assumes that managers choose the sources of finance with the lowest intermediation costs and agency costs. First, companies favor self-financing, i.e. internal financing. It does not require the submission of a file or any negotiation with third parties. In addition, dividend payment targets are tailored according to their investment opportunities. Then, depending on the year, if the results and opportunities are variable, companies use their cash flow. If the financing needs of investments exceed the amount of self-financing, companies resort to external financing. They first choose to issue low-risk debt, i.e. with guarantees for lenders. Likewise, if companies cannot call on traditional debt, they issue debt securities (from the less risky to the riskier). Finally, if the sources cited above prove to be insufficient, companies issue shares and carry out capital increases.

Agency theory takes place in a context of information asymmetry. The agency relation is a contract by which one person (the principal) appoints another person (the agent) to perform certain tasks. This contract implies that the principal delegates part of their decision-making authority to the agent. This relationship is problematic since the interests of the two parties are different. This produces a number of costs that are necessary for executives, for example, to behave in the best interests of the shareholders who appointed them. Agency theory is an attempt to draw a parallel between financial theory and the theory of organizations.

Agency costs can be due to debt. Indeed, in the situation of nearly reaching bankruptcy, a company with debt may accept risky, unprofitable projects (the net present value or NPV is negative), which reduces its value. This practice implies an increase in the value of equity at the expense of that of debt. Shareholders exclude the capital increase for fear of abandoning their contribution to creditors. However, this recapitalization makes it possible to carry out profitable projects. In this case, the agency costs represent the shortfall resulting from rejecting the project for lack of funding. Managers tend to make decisions in favor of the shareholders. These decisions may take the form of company-funded gifts or restrictions on the research and development budget (in order to optimize the distribution of dividends). These practices weaken the competitiveness of the firm and its ability to generate the cash flows that can be used to repay debt. As a result, lenders increase their requirements (agency costs) and insert protection clauses in their contracts. Smith and Warner (1979) have studied the role of these clauses which protect creditors from deviant behavior by shareholders.

Agency costs of equity are the result of disagreements between providers of capital and managers. They relate to companies with a large number of shareholders, which leads to a disconnect between the ownership and the management of the firm. These conflicts, studied by Jensen and Meckling (1976), are due to decisions taken by managers to the detriment of stakeholders. This may be excessive compensation and the allocation of benefits in kind, or inefficient use of surplus cash, instead of increasing the distribution of dividends. This results in the acquisition of marketable securities, whose NPV is equal to 0, that the shareholders could have bought if the company had distributed more dividends or by the acquisition of firms whose activity is not controlled by the company, with the initial aim of diversifying assets. In these cases, the enterprise value falls due to negative NPVs. This decrease corresponds to the agency costs of equity. As Charreaux (1997) explains, shareholders cannot control the deviant behavior of the leaders they have appointed. However, by resorting to debt, which can increase the risk of a company becoming bankrupt, the intention is to support the motivation of managers to make optimal decisions for the company and therefore for its shareholders.

The manager who is not a shareholder seeks to avoid debt which increases the company risk (increase in the breakeven point, financial costs and repayment deadlines that need to be respected) and therefore its own risk (as their income mainly comes from the company). As a precaution, they'll tend to want to accumulate liquidity in the company rather than invest it in risky projects. This behavior is not in the shareholder's interest, as they diversify their assets and perceive the state of being in debt as a stimulus for the manager, and so is encouraged to do their best to free up the cash flow available for the payment of financial expenses and to meet repayment deadlines. In other words, shareholders have an interest in debt to put management under pressure and thereby solve agency problems. The explicit cost of debt constitutes a powerful force impacting the company's management team. Insofar as the parameters of debt are reflected in the company's cash flow while financing via equity results in capital gains or losses at shareholder level, managers have all the more interest in the success of their investments as they are financed by debt. From here, questioning the theory of markets in equilibrium entails a second degree of questioning: the mode of finance influences the choice of investments to the extent that the different forms of finance do not give the same incentives to the business leaders. This means in turn that a company with debt would be more flexible and react faster than a company that is not in debt. The hypothesis has been empirically verified by Ofek (1993). He argues that companies that are listed in the US react (go bankrupt, cut dividends, experience layoffs, etc.) even faster to being in a lot of debt than when they are in a situation of crisis. When it preserves a balanced financial structure, debt is thus one of the modes of internal control that shareholders would choose when it comes to managers[6].

6 The threat of a Public Acquisition Offer is seen as a mode of external control.

In this context, the exercise of business valuation is paramount for each of the stakeholders. Indeed, insofar as a company can buy and be bought, its valuation is of particular interest to investors who look to justify their decision to enter, lend or exit the share, with the manager enabling him/her to position the structure in relation to his/her peers, with the objective of adjusting their management. Therefore, considering the potential value of the company, the market will facilitate the development of financing.

1.3. Valuation measures and follow-up measures

Valuation consists of economically valuing the equity of a company. They can be valued directly or indirectly, i.e. by characterizing the overall value of the company and then deducting the amount of net debt from it in particular. There are three traditional methods.

The comparables method seeks to compare companies or assets of the same nature by focusing on forecasts of aggregates of the income statement and, possibly, of the short-term balance sheet (one or two years of forecast data are necessary as well as aggregates from the last fiscal year). Equity is thus valued by stock market or transactional comparisons.

When the development prospects are considered in the medium or long term, the method of discounted cash flow suggests calculating an intrinsic value of the target company. It results from the calculation of normalized future cash flows from operating income, thus excluding financial expenses, exceptional items and the payment of dividends. Discounting is based on the weighted average cost of capital (WACC). This incorporates the cost of equity and debt found in the CAPM. The value of equity is ultimately obtained by subtracting the value of net debt in particular.

Finally, the proprietary approach evaluates the company as a sum of its assets discounted from net debt. When setting up holding companies, the valuation of revalued net assets recommends restating the equity of hypothetical assets and liabilities before adding unrealized capital gains to them and subtracting unrealized capital losses. In the case of conglomerates, the estimated net assets seek to define, for each branch of activity, an enterprise value obtained by carrying out the assessment presented above. The sum of the various values corresponds to the enterprise value of the conglomerate from which the consolidated net financial debt is deducted to estimate the value of equity. After having evaluated the target, the acquisition can take place on condition that the financing processes have been completed and that the initiator's earnings per share have been assessed, possibly to include the synergies generated by the acquisition.

1.3.1. *Evaluation by comparative approach*

Valuation by stock market comparisons is a method used to determine an objective stock market price of a company and in the context of a public offer when the offer price is presented. It is based on forecasts of financial aggregates. The company is valued for a multiple of its earning capacity, and the markets in equilibrium justify comparisons. This approach is holistic, focusing not on the value of operating assets and liabilities, but on the profitability of their use. The multiple becomes higher as the growth prospects become stronger. The sector of activity is slow risk, and the interest rate charged is low. The valuation of a company is carried out on the basis of a repository of companies that present the same industrial risk. For each of them, multiples of the income statement aggregates are calculated.

This is done by establishing the enterprise value of each company in the sample and relating it to the aggregate in question. Then, an average is taken for each category of multiples. The sector multiples formed from there are applied to the corresponding aggregate from the company that is under valuation. The various corporate values that are then defined are eventually restated, which results in economic values of equity. Depending on the financial specificities of the sector, the relevance of certain multiples will be justified. In addition, these multiples may be taken from a sample of companies that have recently been sold, and for which an equity value has been expressed. Therefore, a company's shares will be valued using the first type of sample if there is no change in control to be noted and a company's equity will be valued using the second type of sample, in case of a change in control. Using the share price to calculate the market multiples provides a "minority" value; the transaction multiples result in "majority" values because they include a control premium. There are two categories of multiples: those that establish enterprise value (multiples of aggregates before financial charges) and those establishing equity (multiples of aggregates after financial charges). Enterprise value EV is the economic value of operating assets. Since the balance sheet is in equilibrium:

$$ASSET = EV + FA \quad [1.56]$$

$$EV = MC + MI + ND - FA \quad [1.57]$$

where:

– MC: market capitalization;

– MI: minority interests;

– ND: net financial debt;

– FA: financial assets.

Enterprise value therefore corresponds to the market value of the industrial and commercial tool. Fixed assets are excluded from this concept insofar as this enterprise value is intended to be compared with sales, gross operating surplus and operating income which do not include financial results. In addition, when restating the enterprise value that makes it possible to economically valuate the shareholders' equity, net debt is notably subtracted, i.e. the financial debt to which investment securities and liquid assets are added. It is therefore necessary to add, during this last step, the financial fixed assets which differ from investment securities only in terms of where they are used. For its part, the net financial debt is made up of all short-, medium- and long-term financial debts, from the value of hedging instruments minus cash flow assets (liquid assets and transferable securities). Theoretically, the value of net debt preserves its market value, i.e. it is equal to the value of future flows to be paid (interest and capital) discounted at the market cost of the debt at which we can subtract the market value of financial investments. We can also use the market value of debts listed and/or traded within an over-the-counter market (bonds, syndications, credit derivatives or CDS). In practice, the market value is often equal to the carrying value (Le Fur and Quiry 2004). The two values are significantly different when:

– the company is indebted at a fixed rate by means of a swap and the interest rates have fluctuated in the meantime;

– the solvency has undergone a significant change after the company has contracted a debt without the interest having been adjusted;

– the nominal rate of the debt has been artificially reduced by the addition of warrants (or other detachable products after the issue).

Finally, market capitalization corresponds to the economic value of equity. If the company is listed, it is equal to the number of shares multiplied by the market price[7].

Throughout this work, the provisions have not undergone any restatement for the following reasons:

– differences in accounting standards IFRS and US GAAP in particular lead to significant discrepancies[8];

– in practice, analysts can assume that they are integrated into the result (thus in equity);

– theoretically, provision for pensions can be assimilated to a financial debt towards employees (Le Fur and Quiry 2003). In practice, analysts can reintegrate it directly into net debt. It is readjusted each year in order to take into account when it is updated[9]. It is similar to a zero coupon bond for which each year the company recognizes an interest charge payable only at the end date. However, if the retirement provision is taken into account when calculating the enterprise value, it is essential to ensure that the EBITDA and the operating profit do not include the fraction of the allowance that corresponds to the passing of time.

And so, the multiple of turnover (TO) shows that the value of operating assets is equivalent to a certain number of times the turnover:

$$x = \text{multiple of TO} = \frac{\text{EV}}{\text{TO}} \quad [1.58]$$

This multiple is of particular interest for a sample which displays a normative and relatively low economic profitability. Otherwise, the results obtained will be heterogeneous. In addition, this multiple makes sense for SMEs for whom turnover is much more indicative of real profitability than the net result published, where transactions are numerous. Finally, this multiple is to be avoided when comparable companies are profitable because

7 If the share is made up of *m* categories of shares where n_k represents the number of shares by *k* and p_k, the category's share price *k*, then the market capitalization equals $\sum_{k=1}^{m} n_k p_k$.

8 Some companies do not have them, while others that belong to the same sector of activity have recorded significant sums which could, therefore, bias the results.

9 The amount of commitment recognized increases each year to the extent that it is an updated amount.

in this case it will tend to overvalue the company. In the equation, by replacing the TO by the EBITDA and by the EBIT, we have:

$$y = \text{multiple of EBITDA} = \frac{\text{EV}}{\text{EBITDA}} \quad [1.59]$$

$$z = \text{multiple of EBIT} = \frac{\text{EV}}{\text{EBIT}} \quad [1.60]$$

The multiple of operating profit makes it possible to enhance the profitability of the company by excluding non-recurring items.

The multiple of gross operating surplus eliminates any significant differences in investment and related repayment choices. The multiple is particularly suited to capital-intensive industries. However, despite the choice of depreciation arrangements, this multiple loses its usefulness in the case where the margin levels of the sample are different.

Companies with low margins are then overvalued, while the opposite effect occurs for those with high margins. P/E is the ratio of the share price to earnings per share. It corresponds to a direct approach[10]:

$$P/E = \frac{\text{price}}{\text{BPA}} = \frac{\text{market capitalization}}{\text{benefactor}} \quad [1.61]$$

Income generated by financial assets is included in net income. In addition, the net result is "shared within the group". This is the reason why no restatement of financial assets and minority interests is to be made.

In practice, net income is restated for non-recurring items and goodwill impairment in order to facilitate an analysis of recurring earning capacity. Indirectly, this multiple based on an aggregate after financial expenses values the financial structure of the company. Thus, if the sample's debt levels are disparate, the valuation may be skewed. This is the reason why, in order to break away from heterogeneous financial structures, the multiple of operating income and, to a lesser extent, that of gross operating surplus are used more.

Based on the estimates of analysts, it is customary to calculate the multiples of comparables on the forecast values of the income statements of companies in the benchmark and the target, always considering the last

10 This equation is systematically applicable even when different share categories are at play.

published financial year. The question then arises as to whether the corporate values should be current (i.e. corresponding to the last published financial year) or whether they can also be forecast. Indeed, the second method fully integrates the investment and financing policy of the company (Le Fur and Quiry 2007). In other words, it seems theoretically irrational to consider, in the multiple of operating income, the investments made in year N+1 (through estimated depreciation) without including in the calculation of the financing linked to these (through "new" equity and/or "new" debt).

By incorporating the notion of forecast value, this method would be granted the ability to differentiate between company multiples with distinct investment and growth profiles. However, the practice tends to go against this reasoning due to the fact that if we were to calculate the value of asset N+1 of the company, we can estimate the net debt N+1. It is, however, impossible to guess the market capitalization N+1. We could propose to capitalize the value of equity N at the cost of capital minus the rate of return.

However, empirically, this method is not used because the market incorporates known future data, through the share price and therefore the market capitalization. Furthermore, the operating profit multiple could be biased if the company is largely financed by debt: the multiple would be unfairly very high. Finally, the other elements allowing the transition from enterprise value to that of equity are most often considered constant because it is difficult to predict. Therefore:

– to value a company in year N+1, it is advisable to keep the same value of the economic assets of the comparable company as for the year N[11]. In any case, the market value of the latter at the valuation date results from the anticipation of how its future operating balances will evolve;

– if a comparable company has a strong investment policy, it is better to exclude it from the sample rather than wanting to wrongly improve the method of evaluating comparables.

The different economic values of equity allow us to compare the company under valuation to its competitors:

– if the value of equity on the basis of the EBITDA multiple is higher than that of turnover, the assessment is more favorable for the company

11 It is also possible to keep this enterprise value in order to realize the multiples of the previous year.

subject to the study since its EBITDA margin is greater than those of its competitors. This point can be verified by comparing the EBITDA margins of the sector with that of the company to be valued;

– if the value of equity on the basis of the multiple of EBIT is higher than that of EBITDA, the valuation is more favorable for the company subject to the study because it has less depreciation and provisions than its competitors. This may reflect a weak investment policy that may reflect a problem of competitiveness;

– if the value of equity based on P/E is greater than that based on EBIT, the valuation is more favorable for the company subject to the study because the leverage effect is used more intensively.

In order to use the transaction multiple method, the sample is built from the information available on transactions observed in the near past in the same sector of activity (among listed and unlisted companies) and from the moment when a change of control has been observed. The acquirer has logically paid an offer price which, in this case, appears as enterprise value.

This price paid incorporates a control premium (of the order of 20–25% of the company's value) which is essential to take possession of the target and which results from a valuation of a share of the anticipated synergies. For each of the companies in the repository, we determine the multiple of turnover, EBITDA, EBIT, P/E of the last financial year closed on the date of the transaction. In other terms, for a transaction carried out in year N, we consider the aggregates of year N-1. For the numerator, the transaction amount replaces the market capitalization. Finally, each average transactional multiple obtained is applied to the homologous aggregate of the company under valuation.

By way of illustration, it was decided that the market comparables method would be applied to value the Royal Dutch Shell company, using a benchmark of companies from the oil industry. Royal Dutch Shell is an Anglo-Dutch company that specializes in energy and petrochemicals. The core business function is to refine and distribute petroleum and natural gas (90% of its turnover at the end of 2013).

The group owns more than 30 refineries and a network of around 44,000 service stations around the world. Around 40% of its activity is carried out in Europe, 35% in Asia-Oceania-Africa and around 25% on the American continent.

On December 5, 2014 (its valuation data), Royal Dutch Shell shares were listed at €27.26 at the opening of the Amsterdam Stock Exchange (AEX Index). Although of different sizes, the companies selected to constitute a reliable repository were Exxon Mobil, Chevron, Conoco Phillips, Petrobras and Total SA.

For the sake of homogenization, the amounts processed – namely the market capitalizations and the data of the balance sheet and income statement aggregates (realized or forecasted) – are expressed in dollars and then, to proceed with the valuation of the share, are quoted in euros, and so a conversion into the European currency is carried out. Moreover, on December 5, 2014, the EUR/USD parity was 1.2282 (parity applied to the benchmark aggregates of Total SA) and the USD/BRL parity was 2.5894 (parity applied to the benchmark aggregates of Petrobras).

Company aggregates for 2013 are taken from financial statements published by oil companies. The 2014 and 2015 forecast data and market capitalization are taken from zonebourse.com.

The multiples of the aggregates of the companies and the average multiples, assimilated to the sector multiples, are shown in Table 1.2.

Applying the average multiples to the corresponding aggregates for Shell finish the valuation[12].

The results of this valuation approach are represented in Figure 1.4.

	Market capitalization (05/12/14)	Net debt	Financial assets	Minority interests	Enterprise value
Exxon Mobil	397,283	18,055	36,328	6,482	385,492
Chevron	209,591	3,915	25,502	1,314	189,318
Conoco Phillips	83,517	15,416	23,907	402	75,428
Petrobras	59,433	94,579	6,666	596	147,942
Total SA	131,990	21,027	18,182	2,802	137,636

12 The amounts on the balance sheet and income statement aggregates from Shell's 2013 registration documents are expressed in dollars. Therefore, the conversion made in Table 1.2 only relates to the final share price since the share listed on the Amsterdam Stock Exchange is expressed in euros.

	Sales			EBITDA			EBIT			Net income		
	2013	2014*	2015*	2013	2014*	2015*	2013	2014*	2015*	2013	2014*	2015*
Exxon Mobil	438,255	417,504	379,124	74,902	72,980	63,016	57,720	54,835	43,024	32,580	32,674	27,706
Chevron	228,848	214,418	184,158	63,154	47,550	42,703	48,968	31,341	24,313	21,423	19,618	16,974
Conoco Phillips	58,248	56,635	54,194	23,455	21,911	20,221	14,446	12,669	9,996	9,156	7,982	6,371
Petrobras	141,462	154,934	164,128	29,426	32,204	39,958	16,083	17,110	22,208	10,832	9,464	13,121
Total SA	232,795	214,493	200,870	35,034	35,408	35,037	24,915	22,754	21,205	10,637	12,720	13,000

*Forecasts zonebourse.com

Table 1.1. *Financial aggregates of the companies in the framework (amounts in millions of $)*

	xSales			xEBITDA			xEBIT			P/E		
	2013	2014*	2015*	2013	2014*	2015*	2013	2014*	2015*	2013	2014*	2015*
Exxon Mobil	0.88	0.92	1.02	5.1	5.3	6.1	6.7	7.0	9.0	12.2	12.2	14.3
Chevron	0.83	0.88	1.03	3.0	4.0	4.4	3.9	6.0	7.8	9.8	10.7	12.3
Conoco Phillips	1.29	1.33	1.39	3.2	3.4	3.7	5.2	6.0	7.5	9.1	10.5	13.1
Petrobras	1.05	0.95	0.90	5.0	4.6	3.7	9.2	8.6	6.7	5.5	6.3	4.5
Total SA	0.59	0.64	0.69	3.9	3.9	3.9	5.5	6.0	6.5	12.4	10.4	10.2
Sector multiple	0.93	0.95	1.00	4.1	4.2	4.4	6.1	6.7	7.5	9.8	10.0	10.9

*Forecasts zonebourse.com

Table 1.2. *Stock market repository of repository companies*

The valuation by the multiple of EBITDA is lower than that resulting from the turnover, given the profitability differential between the sector and Shell, to the detriment of the Anglo-Dutch company. Its EBITDA margin is lower (about 13% for Shell vs. about 24% for the sector). The valuation resulting from the multiple of EBIT is in line with that which results from the multiple of EBIDTA, which comes from an equivalent proportion of depreciation and impairment between the sector and Shell. The valuation by the P/E is lower than that which came from the EBIT. The valuation could improve if the company had recourse to debt, provided that its economic profitability was greater than the cost of its debt. Therefore, it is necessary to exclude the valuation that results from the turnover multiples because the profitability differentials between Shell and its competitors are not taken into account: applying the turnover multiple will overvalue the share.

	xSales			xEBITDA		
	2013	**2014**	**2015**	**2013**	**2014**	**2015**
SHELL Aggregate	451,235	448,379	423,292	59,864	60,436	57,160
SHELL EV	418,643	424,583	425,257	243,244	256,093	250,494
(Net debt 2013)	(34,866)	(34,866)	(34,866)	(34,866)	(34,866)	(34,866)
Financial assets 2013	39,328	39,328	39,328	39,328	39,328	39,328
(Minority interests 2013)	(1,101)	(1,101)	(1,101)	(1,101)	(1,101)	(1,101)
Economic value of equity	*422,004*	*427,944*	*428,618*	*246,605*	*259,454*	*253,855*
Number of shares (millions)	6,371	6,371	6,371	6,371	6,371	6,371
Target share price ($)	66.24	67.17	67.28	38.71	40.73	39.85
Target share price (€)	*53.93*	*54.69*	*54.78*	*31.52*	*33.16*	*32.44*

	xEBIT			P/E		
	2013	**2014**	**2015**	**2013**	**2014**	**2015**
SHELL Aggregate	38,355	33,905	32,781	16,371	21,379	22,088
SHELL EV	233,881	228,654	245,496			
(Net debt 2013)	(34,866)	(34,866)	(34,866)			
Financial assets 2013	39,328	39,328	39,328			
(Minority interests 2013)	(1,101)	(1,101)	(1,101)			
Economic value of equity	*237,242*	*232,015*	*248,857*	*160,416*	*213,627*	*240,663*
Number of shares (millions)	6,371	6,371	6,371	6,371	6,371	6,371
Target share price ($)	37.24	36.42	39.06	25.18	33.53	37.78
Target share price (€)	*30.32*	*29.65*	*31.80*	*20.50*	*27.30*	*30.76*

Table 1.3. *Valuation of Royal Dutch Shell by stock market comparisons (amounts in millions of $)*

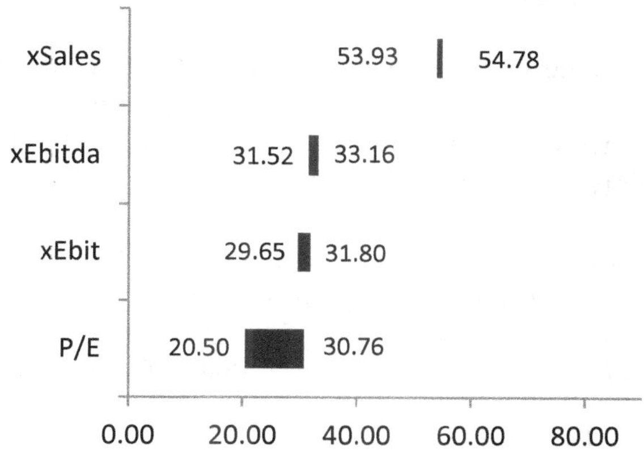

Figure 1.4. *Summary of valuations by stock market comparisons of shares from Royal Dutch Shell (in €)*

In addition, it is wise to rule out the valuation that results from the P/E to the extent that any leverage effect is taken into account in a context where financial structures are heterogeneous. Thus, market capitalizations, which are too disparate between Shell's competitors, do not constitute a relevant benchmark. The target price therefore corresponds to the average of the valuations that result from the EBITDA and EBIT multiples for 2013, 2014 and 2015. Based on the market comparables method and the price on December 5, 2014 (€27.26), the share appears to be undervalued. According to the study carried out, in the medium term, the upside potential may lead the share to list €31.48, i.e. an equity valuation of €200,569 million or $246,338 million (market capitalization on December 5, 2014 is €175,569 million or $215,634 million).

The method used in this application, based on short- and medium-term forecasts, excludes the potential for business development and improvement of long-term profitability. The discounted cash flow (DCF) approach allows us to assess the economic value of operating assets over a much broader space and timeframe using a financing plan. In other words, it is about finding the enterprise value that comes from the sum of the discounted future free cash flows (FCF) generated by the activity of the company to be valued.

1.3.2. *Flow assessment*

The economic value of equity can be obtained following two methods. The first consists of considering that the income of a company's shareholder is made up of dividends received and the market value of the shares that are on resale. Therefore, enterprise value should be based on the sum of the future dividend flows payable by the enterprise and the market value of the stocks at the end of the expected space–time horizon. The second method for obtaining the economic value of equity consists first of estimating the value of the economic asset before subtracting from it the amount of net debt as well as minority interests, before adding the value of fixed assets.

1.3.2.1. *Dividend discount model*

Assuming that the expected space–time frame is infinite, the dividend discount model will not incorporate capital gains since it does not affect the valuation of the share. This notion is thus formalized and an intrinsic value of the company is defined as the present value of future dividends discounted at the cost of equity. Thus, we have:

$$V_0 = \sum_{t=1}^{+\infty} \frac{D_t}{(1+k)^t} \qquad [1.62]$$

where:

– V_t: intrinsic value of equity in time *t*;

– D_t: dividends expected at the period of time *t* (with information being available at the time t-1);

– *k*: cost of equity given the CAPM formula.

Let's assume that the dividends have an annual growth rate *g*:

$$D_t = D_{t-1} + g.D_{t-1} = D_{t-1}(1+g) = D_1(1+g)^{t-1} \qquad [1.63]$$

And so:

$$V_t = D_1(1+g)^{-1} \sum_{t=1}^{+\infty} \left(\frac{1+g}{1+k}\right)^t \qquad [1.64]$$

Knowing that:

$$\sum_{t=1}^{+\infty} q^t = \lim_{n\to+\infty} \sum_{t=1}^{+\infty} q^t = \lim_{n\to\infty} q\frac{1-q^n}{1-q} = \frac{q}{1-q} \quad [1.65]$$

because if $0 < q < 1, \lim_{n\to\infty} q^n = 0$.

Here:

$$q = \frac{1+g}{1+k} \text{ with}^{16}\ g < k \text{ and } g > 0 \text{ and } k > 0 \text{ so } 0 < \frac{1+g}{1+k} < 1 \quad [1.66]$$

We therefore have the formula expressed by Gordon and Shapiro (1959):

$$V_0 = \frac{D_1}{k-g} \quad [1.67]$$

Applied when the company to be valued operates in a mature sector with good visibility (public services, real estate companies, etc.) with a high dividend distribution rate, this method nevertheless has the weakness of not taking into account the organic growth via resources set aside. In practice, many younger companies with high growth potential tend to keep most of their profits or, with a finite forecast horizon, they have no intention of paying dividends. Therefore, the market values of this type of company are larger than those found through the Gordon and Shapiro equation. What is more, according to Modigliani and Miller (1963), the value of a share is not linked to the date that the dividends were paid. It is not uncommon to come across a company that is borrowing funds in the markets in order to be able to remunerate its shareholders, this all being without any apparent link with operating activities or with an investment policy which has created value. The DDM thus focuses on distributing money to shareholders by assuming a consistent distribution without necessarily having any link to the creation of value.

1.3.2.2. *Discounted cash flow model*

The economic value of operating assets results from calculating the enterprise value. It corresponds to the sum of the discounted future free cash flows that have been generated. Subsequently, the net debt and minority

16 Generally, $g \in [0; 4\%]$ and $k \in [8; 15\%]$. In other terms, for the model to work properly, it is essential for the rate of return expected by shareholders is greater than the rate of growth of dividends.

interests are subtracted from it, then financial fixed assets are added to it. We can then obtain the economic value of the equity. In order to find the value of the operating economic asset in the first place, we may apply the technique of choosing the investments that are based on some sort of reasoning:

– in terms of cash flow and not in terms of accounting results. This makes it possible to take into account the variation in the working capital requirement, i.e. the impact of payment delays. In addition, depreciation is calculated according to tax and accounting rules and does not always correspond to an economic reality. An amount only costs or yields at the very time of disbursement or collection, regardless of the treatment given to it. Beyond that, the reasoning is carried out more in terms of opportunity than accounting. Indeed, the account or historical value is of no interest except for tax purposes to know the tax paid on capital gains or tax credits obtained in the event of book value losses. The asset has value, i.e. it corresponds to the acquisition price in the event of investment and to the resale price in the event of divestment;

– in terms of flows induced by operation and investment only. Thus, financing flows are discarded because the cash flows are intended to be discounted at the weighted average cost of capital; the purpose of the calculation being to compare the profitability of investments with the cost of financing. This eliminates financial charges, capital repayments and dividend payments;

– in matters of taxation. Depreciation results in tax savings. The results of the investments are taxed. Depending on the type of investment, the company may benefit from tax credits, allowances, subsidies, etc.

Therefore, the FCF[17] are determined using the taxed operating income (tax is a disbursement). Depreciation (net allocations of reversals), which reduce operating income without reducing cash flow, must be reinstated. In addition, in order to neutralize the receivable income not yet collected and the disbursable expenses not yet disbursed, the change in WCR must be deducted. Finally, net investments of divestments that are not taken into account in the aggregates mentioned constitute disbursements. They must be deducted.

17 FCF = EBIT – IS on the basis of EBIT + depreciations – Δ WCR – investments.

The value of operational assets V equal to the sum of the discounted future FCF is written as so:

$$V = \sum_{t=1}^{n} \frac{FCF_t}{(1+K)^t} + \frac{FCF_n(1+g)}{(1+K)^n(K-g)} \quad [1.68]$$

with:

$$VT = \frac{FCF_n(1+g)}{(1+K)^n(K-g)} \quad [1.69]$$

This method therefore involves determining the cash flows up to infinity. To achieve this, updated forecasts are made over an explicit horizon (5–7 years or even 20–30 years in utilities services) and beyond this horizon, a terminal value is considered[18]. The duration that characterizes the explicit horizon must correspond to the time during which the company will live on its current momentum. If it is too short, the valuation will rely excessively on the terminal value. If it is too long, the valuation will be the subject of a simple theoretical extrapolation. In addition, a growth rate *g* is applied to the final value. At first glance, it is difficult to estimate the terminal value since the date from which it is defined is synonymous with presumption when making forecasts. Therefore, analysts consider that at the end of the explicit horizon, the company has reached its maturity phase. Using the Gordon and Shapiro formula, the most commonly used terminal value is derived from an infinite growth rate *g* applied to a normative flow. The way it can be characterized is the consequence of the investment policy and the evolution of the company's working capital needs. Moreover, it may not be equal to the last flow of the explicit horizon if the activity sector is cyclical because in this case, it would correspond to an average flow generated by the company up to infinity, while the growth forecast for this last year of the business plan would significantly differ from *g*.

However, it is necessary to question the sustainability of market growth and the economic profitability of the company. It would be unfounded to assume a growth rate *g* that is significantly higher than what analysts expect for long-term genuine growth (net after inflation). This would mean that the company to be valued would gain more and more importance in the

18 See the Appendix.

economy over time. The “diminishing rent” model proposes to converge the expected economic profitability of the company towards the cost of capital. This model of cash flow fade makes it possible to create a moment at which the economic profitability deteriorates until it becomes equal to the weighted average cost of capital. This moment would come to pass between the end of the business plan and the terminal value. This can be explained by the decline in margins or by the decline in turnover of economic assets. At the end of the horizon, the final value is equal to the economic asset for its book value. Finally, this model can be applied to a company that is destroying value. In this case, the use of cash flow fade is justified, by assuming that the industry in question cannot remain in the same situation indefinitely. The structural changes, brought about sooner or later by bankruptcies or by market saturation, will make the flows of the company to be valued approach the cost of capital, allowing it to survive (thanks to the growth of economic profitability). Thus, several scenarios can be considered depending on whether we consider the point of view of the prospective buyer or the seller. Negotiations between the two parties will then make it possible to reconcile the valuations of the prices. In practice, the DCF method can be an appropriate dialogue tool. The rate used to discount FCF is the weighted average cost of capital (WACC), which is the weighted average cost of the company’s financial resources. It represents the minimum rate of return required by fund providers to finance the business. This situation results from the “fungibility” of the balance sheet. It is impossible to determine from a company’s accounts the financing of a given asset. Consequently, each asset is financed by equity E and by debt D; the weight of the first and the second in financing each asset corresponds to the weight of each resource in the economic balance sheet of the company. We then have:

$$\mathrm{K} = \mathrm{k}\frac{\mathrm{E}}{\mathrm{E+D}} + \mathrm{i}(1-\mathrm{t})\frac{\mathrm{D}}{\mathrm{E+D}} \qquad [1.70]$$

where:

– K: CMPC;

– *k*: cost of equity;

– *i*: cost of debt;

– *t*: tax rate.

The economic value of the equity required to determine the WACC and therefore the discount rate is precisely what the DCF method should achieve. This is an iterative approach that loops through the value of equity. Approximating a listed company allows us to preserve market capitalization in the WACC formula. Equity value is the difference between EV enterprise value, net financial debt, minority interests, provisions to which financial fixed assets are added. Therefore, maximizing enterprise value through discounting future cash flows leads us to consider the possible existence of an optimal financial structure.

By way of illustration, it was decided that the DCF method would be applied to value the company Royal Dutch Shell. Table 1.4 presents the elements of the financing plan for the Anglo-Dutch company.

In order to extend the business plan from 2017, the assumptions are as follows:

– the growth rate of turnover is estimated at 3% by 2021. Consequently, from 2017 to 2021, there is a linear convergence between the growth rate of the last forecast year (2.2% in 2016) towards the last year of extension (3% in 2021);

– the EBITDA margin rate 2016 (14.1%), the allocations/turnover ratio in 2016 (6.1%) and the corporate tax rate in 2016 (44%) are maintained from 2017;

– the amount of investments in 2021 is equal to the level of allocations planned for the same year ($29,941 million). This results from the assumptions that the company is fully mature by 2021, which then leads it to renew its stock of fixed assets at the rate of its allocations. And so, from 2017 to 2021, there is a linear convergence of the amount of investments for the last forecast year ($34,238 million in 2016) to the level of allocation of the last year of extension ($29,941 million in 2021);

– the WCR is considered to be normative. Consequently, the WCR/turnover ratio observed in 2013 (3.3%) is maintained from 2014 to 2021. From here, we deduce for each year the variation in WCR which comes with the reduction of free cash flows.

	Production	Sourced from zonebourse.com			Extension				
	2013	**2014**	**2015**	**2016**	**2017**	**2018**	**2019**	**2020**	**2021**
Turnover	451,235	448,379	423,292	432,800	443,174	454,465	466,729	480,027	494,428
Growth rate		-0.6%	-5.6%	2.2%	2.4%	2.5%	2.7%	2.8%	3.0%
EBITDA	59,864	60,436	57,160	60,885	62,344	63,933	65,658	67,529	69,555
EBITDA margin rate	13.3%	13.5%	13.5%	14.1%	14.1%	14.1%	14.1%	14.1%	14.1%
(Depreciation allowances)	(21,509)	(26,531)	(24,379)	(26,209)	(26,837)	(27,521)	(28,264)	(29,069)	(29,941)
In % of TO (turnover)	-4.8%	-5.9%	-5.8%	-6.1%	-6.1%	-6.1%	-6.1%	-6.1%	-6.1%
EBIT	38,355	33,905	32,781	34,676	35,507	36,412	37,394	38,460	39,614
(Corporation tax)	(17,066)	(14,918)	(14,424)	(15,257)	(15,623)	(16,021)	(16,454)	(16,922)	(17,430)
Tax rate		44.0%	44.0%	44.0%	44.0%	44.0%	44.0%	44.0%	44.0%
NOPAT	21,289	18,987	18,357	19,419	19,884	20,391	20,941	21,537	22,184
Depreciation allowances	21,509	26,531	24,379	26,209	26,837	27,521	28,264	29,069	29,941
(Net investments)	(40,146)	(33,495)	(33,726)	(34,238)	(33,379)	(32,519)	(31,660)	(30,800)	(29,941)
(DBFR)	(2,988)	94	829	(314)	(343)	(373)	(405)	(439)	(476)
FCF	(336)	12,117	9,839	11,076	13,000	15,019	17,140	19,367	21,708
Discount period		1	2	3	4	5	6	7	8
Discounted FCF		11,359	8,646	9,123	10,038	10,872	11,630	12,319	12,944
WCR	14,904	14,810	13,981	14,295	14,638	15,011	15,416	15,855	16,331
WCR/TO	3.3%	3.3%	3.3%	3.3%	3.3%	3.3%	3.3%	3.3%	3.3%

Table 1.4. *Valuation by DCF of Royal Dutch Shell (amounts in millions $)*

Risk-free rate	1.00%
Market risk premium	5.74%
SHELL Beta	1.08
Cost of equity (k)	7.22%
Cost of debt (i)…	
… before tax	4.37%
… after tax	2.45%
Discount rate (WACC = K)	6.73%
Growth rate to infinity (g)	3.00%

Table 1.5. *Determining the weighted average cost of capital of Royal Dutch Shell*

In order to determine the discount rate:

– the risk-free rate (corresponding to the 10-year OAT rate) which was used is 1%[19];

– the market risk premium was obtained by first constituting a benchmark, all sectors of activity combined, of about 300 companies listed on the CAC 40, AEX, DAX, FTSE 100, FTSE MIB, l'IBEX 35, PSI 20, Dow Jones, Nasdaq and Nikkei 225. Then, for each of the companies in the sample, the quotes at the opening of the stock market on December 5, 2014 were retrieved as well as the estimate of the next dividend paid and the beta of the share[20]. Assuming, on the other hand, an infinite growth rate of 3%, the risk premiums for each company were calculated according to the Gordon and Shapiro equation:

$$V_0 = \frac{D_1}{k-g} \text{ et } k = \frac{D_1}{V_0} + g = r_f + \beta_i[E(R_i) - r_f] \quad [1.71]$$

$$E(R_i) - r_f = \frac{\frac{D_1}{V_0} + g - r_f}{\beta_i} \quad [1.72]$$

where:

– V_0: share price *i* on December 5, 2014;

19 Source: banque-france.fr, website of Banque de France.

20 Source: zonebourse.com and fr.investing.com.

– D_1: estimate of the next dividend paid linked to the share *i*;

– β_i: beta of share *i*;

– r_f: risk-free rate;

– $E(R_i) - r_f$: equity market risk premium of share *i*.

The market risk premium is therefore equal to the average of the 300 values thus calculated, i.e. 5.74%;

– the beta of the Royal Dutch Shell share was obtained by establishing a repository of companies belonging to the same sector of activity as the Anglo-Dutch company. The oil companies chosen are Exxon Mobil, Chevron, Conoco Phillips, Petrobras and Total SA. For each of them, the (indebted) beta of the shares was recovered as well as the net debt and market capitalization[21]. Then, for each of the companies in the benchmark, the debt-free beta was calculated using Hamada's formula (1972):

$$\beta_i^* = \frac{\beta_i}{1+\frac{D(1-\tau)}{E}} \quad [1.73]$$

	Beta	Net debt	Equity	Debt-free beta
Exxon Mobil	0.9	18,055	397,283	0.88
Chevron	1.15	3,915	209,591	1.14
Conoco Phillips	1.07	15,416	83,517	0.97
Petrobras	1.83	94,579	59,433	0.97
Total SA	1.11	21,027	131,990	1.02

Table 1.6. *Indebted beta of companies in the benchmark*

The average debt-free beta (0.99) corresponds to the debt-free beta in the sector. Finally, the following is applied to the financial structure of Royal Dutch Shell:

$$\beta_i = \overline{\beta_i^*}\left[1 + \frac{D(1-\tau)}{E}\right] \quad [1.74]$$

21 Source: zonebourse.com and fr.investing.com for betas and market capitalizations; reference documents for companies for net debt.

The (re)indebted share of Royal Dutch Shell is at 1.08;

– the cost of equity (7.22%) is obtained by applying the CAPM formula;

– the cost of debt is determined according to the Standard & Poor's debt rating guide. As of January 17, 2014, Shell bonds are rated according to the AA rating agency and the associated cost of debt is 4.37% before IS (i.e. 2.45% after tax);

– the FCF is discounted using the weighted average cost of capital (6.73%) by performing an iterative calculation of the WACC (closure on the desired value);

– the infinite growth rate (3%) is the assumed rate, in accordance with the assumption made in corporate and investment banks, and is in line with the method for determining the market risk premium.

The 2013 balance sheet shows a net financial debt of $34.9 billion. Enterprise value ($298.6 billion) is equal to the sum of discounted FCF over the business plan period ($86.7 billion) and the terminal value ($211.9 billion). The economic value of equity ($302 billion) is obtained by deducting new debt, minority interests and auditing financial assets to the enterprise value. Shell's target price is thus $48.4 or €38.59 (the stock market price is €27.26 on the valuation date, December 5, 2014).

Sum of DCFs 2014–2021	86,745
Terminal value	211,855
Enterprise value	298,600
(Net debt)	(34,866)
Fixed assets	39,328
(Minority interests)	(1,101)
Equity	301,961
Number of shares (millions)	6,371
Target price ($)	47.4
Net result 2013	16,371
Implied	18
Target price (€)	38.59

Table 1.7. *Value of equity of Royal Dutch Shell*

		Risk-free rate				
		1.0%	1.5%	2.0%	2.5%	3.0%
Growth rate g	3%	301,961	269,528	243,633	222,521	205,007
	4%	375,621	324,694	286,246	256,259	232,261
	5%	515,810	420,578	355,472	308,274	272,563
	6%	886,304	628,291	487,344	398,781	338,122

Table 1.8. *Sensitivity analysis of the value of Royal Dutch Shell at the risk-free rate and to infinite growth*

Based on the discount rate and perpetual growth rate retained *ad infinitum*, the valuation is between $205 billion and $886 billion. The advantage of this method is to concretely translate the different assumptions and forecasts of buyers and sellers. A certain serenity is maintained in the face of periods of stock market overvaluation. It keeps economic performance grounded in reality. This method, satisfactory in theory, has three major drawbacks, however:

– is it very impacted by the assumptions and objectivity of the person who established it. Therefore, its results are very volatile. This is a rational method that can be biased;

– sometimes, it depends too much on the terminal value, to which the problem is ultimately transferred. Terminal value often explains 50% of the company's value (Vernimmen 2012, p. 743). This can call into question its validity even though, sometimes, it is the only method applicable when the results are negative and the multiples are not applicable;

– it is not always easy to carry out a business plan over a sufficient period of time: the information is often lacking for the external analyst.

The two valuation methods discussed above are based, on the one hand, on a stock market analysis and, on the other hand, on what the asset portfolio would be worth in the future. A third valuation method is to intuitively consider that the business is worth what it owns in reality and instantly.

1.3.3. *Valuation through propriety and mixed approaches*

The propriety methods consist of valuing the assets, divisions or subsidiaries separately, by deducting the commitments of the company. The objective is to correct and reassess book values that are different from the actual values due to the consideration of accounting, tax and historical rules. This valuation method is particularly suitable for conglomerates or groups whose activities are diversified insofar as their accounts and financial projections must be the subject of separate analyses. In fact, the assets valued correspond to subsidiaries for their share of ownership or to branches of activity value separately using the multiples of DCF method. The holding's net debt and the present value of the head office costs then decrease this sum. There are three types of asset values: market value, which represents the value of reselling an asset, the net asset value, which corresponds to the market value minus a discount linked to the need for a quick sale, and the use value, which represents the value of an asset within the operating process. Thus, since several perspectives are possible, the assessment must preserve the consistency of its approach (cessation of activity or continued operation). The value of a company with high asset value can bring about speculation and volatility insofar as the terminal value plays a very important part compared to intermediary flows, considering the DCF method. In other words, the industrial risk may be low, but it causes speculation for the value of resale. Therefore, this valuation method is useful for valuating SMEs with no strategic value or industrial assets for which a secondary market exists.

1.3.3.1. *Revalued net assets*

In order to define the revalued net asset, it is necessary to consider the account net asset which corresponds to the difference between the real assets (assets with a market value) and the real debts. Assets other than real assets are hypothetical assets, i.e. uncalled subscribed capital, start-up costs, research and development costs, bond redemption premiums and accrual-asset accounts (namely charges to be distributed, prepaid charges and rate differences on assets). Hypothetical debts (other than real debts) are accruals and deferred income (i.e. deferred revenues and unrealized foreign exchange)

$$\text{ANC} = \text{real assets} - \text{real debts} \qquad [1.75]$$

$$\text{ANC} = \text{equity} - \text{hypothetical assets} + \text{hypothetical debts} \qquad [1.76]$$

Revalued net assets result from the difference between the economic value of real assets (generally greater than the net book value) and the economic value of real debts (commonly assimilated to their book value)

$$NAV = \text{economic value of real assets} - \text{real debts} \quad [1.77]$$

$$NAV = ANC + PVL \text{ on assets} \quad [1.78]$$

The economic valuation of tangible assets does not mean that it is a matter of breaking down the value of each asset and then adding it up. It is the intrinsic overall value of the industrial and commercial tool that matters. In addition, the stocks of certain companies with a long production cycle may be subject to revaluation in the event of any capital gains noted. In this case, we must also take into account the impact of corporate tax. Finally, intangible assets are subject to specific valuation methods:

– business capital is assessed for SMEs on the basis of scales used by experts and courts as a percentage of turnover. For large groups, it is assessed by discounting the excess profit generated at the economic rate of return given a probable lifespan, depending on an attrition rate;

– trademarks and patients can be valued by considering advertising expenditure post tax.

In addition, a provisional balance sheet must not contain unrealized losses. However, unrealized losses or unrealized capital losses on certain assets must be deducted from the NAV:

$$NAV = ANC + UG - UL \quad [1.79]$$

where:

– UL: unrealized losses;

– UG: unrealized gains.

Taking tax into account implies adopting a certain approach to valuation:

– from a continuity point of view, the tax impact is neglected because the company does not intend to sell the assets that generate capital gains. Thus, latent taxation on capital gains and losses is eliminated;

– from a liquidation perspective, the assets are theoretically sold. Thus, unrealized taxes reduce unrealized capital gains. Likewise, unrealized tax credits reduce unrealized capital losses. In that case:

$$NAV \text{ after } IS = ANC + UG - ISL/UG - UL + \text{eco. from } ISL/UL \quad [1.80]$$

where ISL is the latent corporate tax.

The NAV method serves to value the holdings. Their listed assets are valued on the basis of the stock market price (NAV by market transparency). NAV, after taking into account latent taxation, is also called adjusted net book value (ANBV).

The estimated net assets are used for a conglomerate (its activities are not necessarily subsidiary). The economic value of equity is obtained by the sum of the asset values of each department from which the consolidated net debt (enterprise value) is deducted.

1.3.3.2. *Determining and justifying a difference in value*

Assets useful for operation (fixed assets + current assets)
+ UG – UL
+ Cost of reclamation of useful fixed assets useful for operation
+ Value of goods rented of financed by leasing and useful to operation [1.81]

GSV: gross substantial value
– Current assets
+ WCR

PCV: permanent capital vehicle

The VSB is the economic value of assets that are useful in the day-to-day business of the company, whether the business is the owner or the leaseholder. Thus, fictitious assets, financial fixed assets and marketable securities are excluded. The costs of repairing fixed assets and major repairs that the company will have to make to continue its current activity are assumed to be capitalized and taken into account in the calculation of the VSB. Their depreciation, which is tax deductible, is taken into account in the calculation of the normalized profit. There, it is possible to consider the shortened goodwill annuity to be:

$$V_E = ANBV + GW \quad [1.82]$$

$$GW = \sum_{t=1}^{n} \frac{P - K.GSV}{(1+k)^t} = (P - K.GSV)\frac{1-(1+k)^{-n}}{k} \quad [1.83]$$

where:

$$GW = \sum_{t=1}^{n} \frac{P-K.PCV}{(1+k)^t} = (P - K.PCV)\frac{1-(1+k)^{-n}}{k} \quad [1.84]$$

where:

– P: normalized profit (generated by current activity);

– K: WACC;

– *k*: cost of equity (CAPM).

By noting VR, the return value, the *goodwill* is shown to be, by the German method:

$$VR = \sum_{t=1}^{+\infty} \frac{RN}{(1+k)^t} = \frac{RN}{k} \text{ or } VR = \sum_{t=1}^{+\infty} \frac{Dividend}{(1+k)^t} = \frac{Dividend}{k} \quad [1.85]$$

$$V_E = ANBV + GW = \frac{ANBV+VR}{2} \quad [1.86]$$

$$GW = \frac{VR-ANBV}{2} \quad [1.87]$$

By the Anglo-Saxon method, the number of years of shortened goodwill annuity forecasts tends towards infinity. Respectively, [1.83] and [1.84] become:

$$GW = \sum_{t=1}^{+\infty} \frac{P-K.VSB}{(1+k)^t} = \frac{P-VSB}{k} \quad [1.88]$$

$$GW = \sum_{t=1}^{+\infty} \frac{P-K.PCV}{(1+k)^t} = \frac{P-K.PCV}{k} \quad [1.89]$$

By way of illustration, the proprietary approach was applied by value of the company Royal Dutch Shell. The elements in Table 1.9 can be referred to in order to value the Anglo-Dutch company.

The proprietary approach greatly overestimates the economic value of equity. Royal Dutch Shell, whose market capitalization on December 5, 2014 is €175,569 million (or $215,634 million), has invested in profitable assets.

The practice of valuation is particularly useful in the market for corporate control. The shareholder analysis precedes the valuation of the company with a view to control operations. The latter defines the strategy of the company. It is then a question of clarifying the distribution of power between the shareholders and the managers of the company. To the extent that the shareholders control the structure, questions may arise in terms of objectives, notably concerning their personal gains and keeping their jobs. The study of the geography of capital, i.e. the distribution of power between the different shareholders, differs depending on whether the company is listed or not. Within a company that is not listed, agreements between owners of capital are governed, conferring a certain balance. Under these conditions, an external diagnosis may prove unsuccessful if the analyst ignores the implications of these shareholder agreements. A shareholder's agreement is a legal document signed between several shareholders making it possible to govern their relationships over time. They revolve around governance clauses (distribution of director and management positions, general voting conditions, etc.) and changes in the shareholding structure (temporary non-transferability clause, pre-emption in the event of sale, etc.).

	Asset			Passive	
Amount (millions of dollars)	**VNC**	**Economic value**	**Value retained for the VSB**		
Software	1,831	1,831	1,831	**Equity**	181,148
Goodwill	2,563	0	0	**Provisions**	34,509
Fixed assets	191,897	371,115	371,115	**Financial debt**	44,562
Equity securities	39,328	39,328	0	**Payables**	74,177
Stocks	30,009	30,009	30,009	**Social and tax debts**	23,116
Receivables	39,094	39,094	39,094	**Other debts**	0
Tax and social receivables	5,785	5,785	5,785		
Other receivables	37,309	37,309	0		
VMP	4,890	4,890	0		
Liquid assets	4,806	4,806	4,806		
Total	357,512	534,167	452,640	**Total**	357,512

Table 1.9. *2013 balance of Shell and values used to determine its VSB*

To determine Shell's VSB, assets that do not fall within the scope of operation should be excluded and the economic value of the buildings should be retained. Thus, the value of the permanent capital necessary for the operation is defined as so:

Balance sheet value retained for the VSB	452,640
Rented equipment	32,541
VSB	485,181
Operation working capital requirements	(22,405)
(Current operating assets)	(74,888)
PCV	387,888

Table 1.10. *Determining Shell's PCV*

Valuation by proprietary approach is shown in Table 1.11.

Net result	16,526
IS	17,066
Net financial expenses	4,763
Normalized profit before IS	38,355
(IS)	(16,876)
Normalized IS net profit	21,479
WACC	6.68%
P-K.PCV	(4,432)
k (CAPM)	7.22%
Rate of negative goodwill	(61,387)
ANR (continuity of operation)	392,312
Economic value of equity ($)	330,925
Number of shares (millions)	6,371
Target price ($)	51.94
Target price (€)	42.29

Table 1.11. *Determining the economic value of equity of Shell*

1.4. The perspectives of assessment: control operations

Control operations are closely linked to shareholding. Thus, there are different strategies for acquiring or consolidating control which depend on the nature of the composition of the holders of the company's capital as well as the level at which the latter are situated in the development cycle of the company. The resulting control negotiations are subject to specific regulations and impact the company's aggregates. Finally, financial agreements such as the LBO (leverage buy out) which is based on the benefits linked to the use of leverage, show us that the offer price is the result and not the hypothesis. Indeed, the sale price of the target company is equal to the amount of funds that the takeover holding company can raise.

1.4.1. *The shareholder*

A family shareholding grouped together in a common holding company or a foundation is distinguished from the business angles in which former managers and shareholders of companies invest and provide assistance through their interactions with start-up companies. Investment funds or private equity, on the other hand, are financed by insurance companies, pension funds or high net worth individuals. They are specialized according to the objective of their intervention corresponding to different stages of maturity of the company:

– venture capital funds finance early companies that do not yet have access to financial markets and for which debt is not desirable. Seed capital or reversal capital is found, which corresponds to the recovery of businesses;

– development capital funds become shareholders of companies which are experiencing strong growth and which have high financing needs;

– leverage buyout funds have exclusive control over the company given the significant risk taken through the leverage effect. The stock market listing is somewhat antagonistic, especially as these funds seek fiscal integration between the takeover holding company and the target company. These funds are sometimes introduced on the stock exchange.

These investment funds are managed for a limited life (maximum 10 years) after which they are liquidated. The company is ultimately sold or listed on the stock market.

A shareholding which brings together institutional investors, i.e. banks, insurance companies, pension funds, or mutual funds generally hold a minority stake (less than 10% of the capital) of listed companies. However, since they constitute the bulk of the float, they define the market value of the company. Employee share ownership results from the participation of employees in the capital of the company. It is a pillar of stability that strengthens the position of the main shareholder. In France, this often takes the form of a company savings plan. Finally, the state shareholder experiences temporary revivals when it comes to preventing companies from going bankrupt or subscribing to capital increases to help them through a negative stage.

The shareholders seek to establish their control over the company, especially if it is listed. The anti-takeover defenses consist first of splitting the power of capital. The setting up of shares with double voting rights falls within a specific regulatory context following their inclusion in the articles of association following the deliberation of a significant general meeting. The shares are registered, which ensures a certain knowledge of the shareholders and protects the company from a takeover bid in the short term to the extent that potential buyers would have to reveal themselves to benefit from the share. Moreover, by increasing the number of minority shareholders, the formation of holding aims to preserve control of the company. Finally, the limited partnership by shares fully separates the management from the holding of capital.

The shareholders of a company defend themselves against potentially hostile transactions by granting themselves control rights. Therefore, by granting their own right to approval, they can avoid the emergence of an unwanted partner and the pre-emption clause gives a category of shareholders the right to become a priority purchaser when it is put up for sale.

Shareholder defense strategies can also intervene through their consolidation. Therefore, a reserved capital increase (in cash or in kind) requires the waiver of the shareholders who subscribe to their preferential subscription right. In the event that the company is listed, the subscription price must be greater than the stock market price. Even though the merger takes place for strategic reasons, in terms of control, it results in a reserved capital increase. This is because it allows for the introduction of new shareholders or the consolidation of old ones. In the same way, a company can buy back part of their shares from its shareholders with the objective of canceling them out. Finally, by issuing share warrants, the company protects itself in the event of an external threat, insofar as the investors then holding these securities exercise them and thus become shareholders.

These provisions designed to protect shareholders against hostile public offerings only make sense if the company has gone public. By going through the primary market, it opens its capital to the public and collects money. The goal is to develop the entity and to internationalize it by accessing new markets (internal growth), or by buying other companies (external growth), to allow the initial partners to sell all or part of their shares with a view to realize capital gains and integrate significant financial collaborators. The IPO can also take advantage of the notoriety it is able to generate. As the company that is then listed is visible on the market, which means that they can benefit from a genuine sense of publicity, they are able to find quality partners and to attract and retain quality personnel through stock options and incentives, for example.

The stock market listing allows us to access the capital market, while enabling the value of the company to be externalized. Therefore, this entails a certain level of speed when investing funds, compared to when one obtains private financing due to the existence of financial analyst services. The latter publish studies that influence the rationality of markets. In addition, the information is made public due to the reference documents that are available in France on the AMF website. This listing logic allows CFOs to sell the business in the form of securities placed solely on the basis of profitability and risk criteria. Consequently, mismanagement will be punished by a poor performance of the share price, which can actually result in a hostile takeover bid. In theory, the shareholder is able to find liquidity in the stock market. This is why the IPO issue seems to be more of a shareholder issue rather than a company-wide issue. In practice, this can be concluded for the top 200 listed companies. Beyond this supposed liquidity, the minority shareholder will find projections that no convention offers, which are based on expressing interest in the listing. Indeed, the company has an obligation to inform itself and it must develop a coherent dividend distribution policy. The majority shareholder, on the other hand, is not able to devise a strategy that is decorrelated from financial parameters such as growth rate or earnings per share.

Asker *et al.* (2011) empirically demonstrate that unlisted companies invest more than listed companies and that they are more responsive to investment opportunities due to the lucidity of their shareholders. For the company, the stock market listing is beneficial in terms of its notoriety. Indeed, successful financial communication can attract quality partners (customers, suppliers, employees via stock option and incentive plans, etc.)

and generate a level of positive publicity on the international stage. In addition to this, a listing can provide a rapid measurement of business performance and, due to the easier access to information, the business can diversify its sources of finance and reduce its debt costs.

Beyond the choice of one or more rarely multiple places where the listing appears, the IPO requires us to establish several parameters such as the size of the IPO and the choice of operation. The latter can be primary, i.e. synonymous with a capital increase, secondary, or synonymous with transferring shares by the shareholders that are in place, or mixed, i.e. in the presence of two operations. The sizing is then carried out according to:

– the desire of current shareholders to monetize all or part of their stake;

– the company's need for capital to finance its growth;

– the need to be rid of debt;

– the need to offer the market an adequate volume of securities so that the share can offer sufficient liquidity without running the risk of sending a negative message to players.

The constraints described must be considered globally. Indeed, if shareholders wish to sell all of their securities, the market may sense a negative signal. In addition, a capital increase connotes more optimism insofar as the market can foresee wide possibilities for the company to develop. In fact, in this case, it calls on a new source of funding. Technically, while waiting for the registration request to be gone through with the supervisory authorities (the AMF in France)[22], the company and its subscribers are considering the issue price. Underwriters are the financial intermediaries who provide the company with valuable procedural and financing advice. They buy the securities themselves before reselling them to the public. So, to set the offer price, they look at the P/Es of major competitors and then perform discounted cash flow calculations. The various presentation sessions with potential investors and the understanding of their intentions to purchase, in terms of price or maximum amount to be invested, make it possible to draw up the status of potential orders. After receiving authorization from the supervisory authorities, the company sets the issue

22 The request identifies information on the proposed financing, the history of the company, its current activity and its plan for future development (document the main parts of which are distributed to investors in the form of a prospectus).

price. Purchasers are then responsible for successfully selling all the securities to the public. They take the risk that the issue will fail and end up with unsold securities.

Guarantees can be contractualized. For example, we can commit to sell a maximum number of shares without ensuring a full sale. The threefold role of subscribers generates renumeration that results from commissions in the form of a spread. Purchasers then buy the shares at a price lower than the offer price to investors. In the riskier cases, purchasers receive additional non-cash compensation, such as warrants in order to purchase other securities at a later date. Since most underwriter costs are fixed, the percentage spread decreases with the size of the issue. Chen and Ritter (2000) note that the bulk of introductions between €20 and 80 million earn 7%. They explain this constancy of the spread by claiming that the underwriting market is not competitive, which Hansen (2001) denies. In addition to the subscription costs, the company which proceeds to its IPO must pay significant administrative costs that result from preparing the registration document and the prospectus (legal advisors, accountants, management, underwriters, advisors, etc.), registration fees relating to the issuance and costs related to the printing and the delivery of mail in particular. The costs of undervaluation also exist. Indeed, we must not overlook the business that can be achieved by investors who subscribed to the IPO and realized a capital gain shortly after the transaction at the expense of the initial shareholders. These costs, which are hidden but very significant, can far exceed the costs of issuance mentioned above. A study by Ibboston *et al.* (1994) and subsequently updated[23] shows that out of 15,000 issues from 1960 to 2003, there is an average undervaluation of about 19% at the end of the first day of listing. The study also distinguishes disparities by country. For example, in China, the gains from an acquisition at the time of the IPO reach an average profitability of 250%, while in France, it is around 15%[24]. Investment bankers and institutional investors argue that undervaluation can be beneficial to the issuing firm, considering that a low issue price increases the price of the security when it is a result of a significant trading on the secondary market, therefore increasing the company's ability to raise other capital. The analysis of how companies can rationally undervalue their issue price in order to facilitate their dissemination to the public is repeated in the work of Welch (1989).

23 Via the website: http://bear.cba.ufl.edu/ritter.

24 These are category A domestically traded shares.

Another point of view relating more to behavioral finance should be brought out here. This point of view deals with the phenomenon of the "winner's curse": the most relentless bidder in a sale (whatever that sale may be) is also the one who has seemed to overestimate the value of the property. If we were to translate this to the IPO, an investor could, in theory, participate in all IPOs. It would be simple for them to own shares coming from issuances that no one cares about. Conversely, assuming that the issuance is popular, underwriters will not be able to satisfy all investors for lack of shares. Therefore, the strategy of the investor in question may result in the loss of money. In short, in order to make gains, the investor would only invest if the undervaluation is on average consistent. As a result, ill-informed investors cannot distinguish between good and bad issues that are relating to the "winner's curse". Companies and their underwriters would be aware of this, and would endeavor to offer an average undervaluation in order to attract uninformed investors. It must be said that this phenomenon can only justify part of the phenomenon of undervaluation, and certainly not Chinese issuances. Finally, Loughram and Ritter (2002) insist on another behavioral bias. In the mind of the initial shareholder, who should, *a priori*, feel irritated by an undervaluation during an IPO, this is an entirely distinct phenomenon. The cost of undervaluation would be offset by the discovery of greater wealth than expected. Indeed, it should be kept in mind that in general, shareholders do not part with all of their shares, if any at all. For example, Pierre Omidyar, principal shareholder, founder and CEO at eBay's IPO, has retained his entire portfolio of 15.2 million shares. The prospectus for the initial offering proposed to sell 3.5 million shares between $14 and $16. However, with the buzz the company generated, underwriters raised the issue price to $18 and sold 4.5 million shares. At the close of the second day, the stock was trading at $47.375. We could then imagine Pierre Omidyar's frustration with such a situation where his company's securities were grossly undervalued. But we should not forget that the increase from $18 to $47.375 results in an increase in his wealth by $447 million. Thus, undervaluation cannot always be negatively perceived by the shareholder, who gets richer as the stock price rises.

The listed or unlisted status of a company and the inclination of the former shareholders to subscribe to the operation determine the investment technique during capital increase. When the company is listed, we can expect more existing shareholders to participate in the capital increase; due to a desire not to bring in new sources of equity, the technique is carried out with preferred stock purchase rights (PSPR). The operation takes place over

5 days at least, after having fixed and announced an issue price for the new shares at a discount to the stock market price of around 15–30% in normal market conditions (in 2009, some discounts reached 50% of the share price). The aim is thus to avoid a situation where the operation fails if a drop in the price on the secondary market occurs during the subscription period. In order not to disadvantage current shareholders, a negotiable preferred stock purchase right is available during the entire transaction. It corresponds to a right attached to each old share, which allows its holder to subscribe to the issuance of new shares. In fact, current shareholders can subscribe to new financial securities in proportion with their existing level of participation in the business. If their stock rights have been fully used, they will remain indifferent to the price at which the transaction takes place. If among these same shareholders, it turns out that some do not wish to subscribe to the capital increase, the preferred stock purchase rights can be sold separately from the old shares held. This transferable right thus makes it possible to adjust the issuance price to the market value of the share. It is similar to a purchase option in which the underlying is the share, the exercise price corresponds to the issue price of the new shares and the duration is that of the period of the operation. The value of a stock purchase right must be such that after the capital increase, a shareholder who held an old share and who has sold the attached right must be in the same financial situation as an investor who buys a new share and the preferred stock purchase rights within the parity report of the issuance:

$$\mathrm{X} - \mathrm{PSPR} = \mathrm{Y} + \frac{\mathrm{x}}{\mathrm{y}}\,\mathrm{PSPR} \qquad [1.90]$$

$$\mathrm{PSPR} = \frac{\mathrm{X}-\mathrm{Y}}{1+\frac{\mathrm{x}}{\mathrm{y}}} \qquad [1.91]$$

where:

– X: value before issuance (old stock market price);

– Y: issuance price;

– x: number of old shares;

– y: number of new shares;

– PSPR: value of the preferred stock purchase rights.

Let P be the theoretical course of the share after the operation. P is at:

$$P = X - PSPR \quad [1.92]$$

The detachment of subscription rights is similar to the distribution of free shares. Furthermore, if the former shareholder wishes to carry out a cash-neutral transaction, i.e. to keep the same assets (in terms of amount) before and after the capital increase, they must determine the number of new shares to which they will subscribe and the number of preferred stock purchase rights to be transferred. Thus, either:

– M: amount of wealth before and after the operation;

– *i*: number of shares held before the operation;

– *j*: number of new shares to which the old shareholder must subscribe;

– *n*: number of preferred stock purchase rights to sell.

The amount of wealth M before the operation can be expressed as:

$$M = X.i \quad [1.93]$$

The amount of wealth M after the operation can be expressed as:

$$M = (i + j).P \quad [1.94]$$

where:

$$j = \frac{M}{P} - i \quad [1.95]$$

The number of preferred stock purchase rights, *n*, to sell in order to not change the value of wealth before and after operation is at:

$$n.PSPR = j.Y \quad [1.96]$$

where:

$$n = \frac{j.Y}{PSPR} \quad [1.97]$$

If one expects that the current shareholders will only subscribe in a minority group to a capital increase, or if the company wishes to initiate a process of enlarging its shareholder base, the operation is carried out without preferred stock purchase rights. Former shareholders may possibly benefit from a priority period. Moreover, the issuance price comes after a period of marketing and pre-preparation. The discount is not significant compared to the market price. The role of the banking syndicate is all the more important insofar as marketing efforts must be made to convince investors to become shareholders. A guaranteed investment is then dependent on the technique used.

For a company that carries out a capital increase, the benefit lies in the reduction of the debt ratio since we may witness an increase in shareholders' equity that runs concomitantly with a decrease in net financial debt, considering the injection of cash flow. The downside is the decrease in earnings per share, and the possibility that the transaction will not be possible if the nominal value goes above the stock price, or will fail entirely if the stock price after the transaction falls below the stock market price.

At any given time, a single company can have several values assigned to it. This results from the difference between the differing objectives of potential buyer(s) and seller(s), as well as their respective expectations for future results and synergies. Consequently, negotiations may begin and the transaction can be successful as long as the positions of the different actors are reconcilable. In other words, the value of synergies between buyer and seller must be shared so that they can each derive relative satisfaction.

1.4.2. *Control negotiations*

Change of control transactions is undertaken in cash or in securities. These are usually distributed at high valuations, in order to avoid any potential issues with absolute values. The 1990s and 2000s were characterized by globalization and sectoral saturation after we witnessed, in the 1960s, more conglomerate logics (Fiat, Schneider, etc.) where the parent companies give capital globally to their subsidiaries acquired in shares and, in the 1980s, to a level of debt which is a by-word for the financing of more acquisitions. The conglomerates that were revered in the 1960s then fell into decline, to the extent that they were valued less than the sum of the values of the whole group. Consequently, for the last 20 years, mergers have mainly been paid in shares (GDF-Suez, BNP Paribas-Fortis, Arcelor-Mittal, etc.). Shleifer and Vishny (1997) justify this evolution by looking at the emergence of undervalued and overvalued companies which coexist at the same time. The latter try to acquire the former by buying undervalued assets which allows them to consolidate their own value, limiting its rate decline as the market becomes aware of their overvaluation. The phenomenon subsides when the undervalued companies have all been bought out (late 1980s) and/or when the overvalued companies undergo a rebalancing of value (early 2000s).

In addition, macroeconomic elements can be added to these financial considerations. In fact, mergers between companies take place more during phases of technological evolution and innovation: at this point in time, we witness numerous foundations of new companies which, subsequently, become saturated due to the reduction in growth prospects. What is more, their significant needs for financing – linked, for example, to market extensions or increased competition that entails rapid growth – require that they reach a critical size, which limits any room to maneuver if these companies do not join a particular group. In addition, the preponderance of financial markets in a liberal and deregulated economy – compared to the 1980s in particular – generates a disintermediation between companies and providers of funds, which is synonymous with an increase in power of the shareholders over managers. It results in a sense of pressure experienced by the latter to satisfy a suitable level of profitability, with the risk that in the event of poor performance, the massive resale of shares will lead to a drop in the stock market price, thus favoring a public takeover bid or exchange. Finally, microeconomic elements are critical. Unit costs may decrease if the size and volumes of production are increased. Therefore, an acquisition allows companies to benefit from economies of scale in terms of research/development, management and distribution costs, as well as an increased bargaining power with suppliers, allowing them to lower procurement costs. In addition, company mergers are synonymous with market share gains and the maximization of group revenues. This may be, regarding synergies, the elimination of a competitor or even the reduction of debt.

The analysis of research work, which retrospectively determines the creation or destruction of value generated by acquisition operations, is necessary to conduct in order to then focus on the distribution of the creation of value among the shareholders of the acquirer and those of the target company. The premium paid is a source of value creation for the target's shareholder. However, since the 2000s, the shareholders of acquirers benefit from only one-third of value creation. The quality and speed of the process of integrating the target into the group is an overriding factor in the success or failure of the merger.

1.4.2.1. *Regulation of public offers*

In its regulations, the AMF[25] sets out the procedure to be carried out and the process that results from a merger between listed companies. The launch of the offer is part of a normal or simplified procedure. The initiator may increase their previous offer by facing a stock market battle in the event of the emergence of a competing offer. In addition, the public tender offer and the public exchange offer may be followed by a public buyout offer or even a "squeeze-out".

A public offer begins with the filing of a document by the financial institution that presents the offer to the AMF. It includes a letter that describes the objectives and the intentions of the initiator, the number and nature of the securities of the target company already held (in isolation or together) or which may be held at its sole initiative, the date and the conditions of the possible acquisition or already completed acquisition, the price (in the case of a public tender offer) or the exchange parity with a view to the acquisition (in the case of a public exchange offer), the elements used to set them out and the predicted payment or exchange conditions, possibly the conditions before the completion of the operation[26], copies of the draft prospectus and prior declarations made to the bodies permitted to authorize the planned transaction.

Once the proposed offer is filed, the listed price of the securities of the target company may be suspended by the AMF[27]. It then makes the main provisions of the draft offer public. The offer period ends when the results are published. The AMF has 5 days to examine its admissibility, from the

25 http://www.amf-france.org.

26 The precedent condition may be linked to obtaining securities (expressed as a percentage of the capital or voting rights), at the end of the transaction. Furthermore, if the same initiator files various draft offers on separate companies, there may be an obligation to obtain a threshold for holding capital or voting rights on some or all of the target companies. Under merger control, if the proposed public offer is the subject of a notification to the European Commission, the Minister of the Economy or the competent authority of a Member State of the European Union or the United States, it is necessary to obtain the decision provided for in Article 6-1 (a) or (b) of Regulation (CEE) no. 4064/89, the authorization provided for in Article L. 430-5 of the French Commercial Code or any similar authorization issued by the institution in question.

27 This suspension may also affect other securities affected by the proposed offer.

opening of the regulated market once the filing of the draft offer has been published. It is also required to ask the presenting institution for all appropriate justifications and guarantees, as well as any other information necessary for its assessment[28]. The admissibility of the proposed offer is assessed following the examination of the objectives and intentions of the initiator, the price or the exchange parity, the evaluation criteria used, the characteristics of the target company, the nature, the characteristics, the share price or the market of the securities offered in exchange and the precedent conditions set by the initiator in terms of the holding threshold.

The AMF then publishes its decision and sets the date for resuming negotiations for the securities concerned. The proposal may consist of a single offer (e.g. purchase of the securities concerned or exchange for securities issued or to be issued or payment in securities and in cash), an alternative offer or a main offer accompanied by a subsidiary option. The initiator may allow the holders to proceed with the deferred sale of their securities. Any formula that consists of proposing maturity payment of the difference between the market price and the price put forward must include guarantees and advantages that are equivalent to those relating to the deferred sale.

The normal procedure applies when the initiator acts alone or with others and holds less than half of the capital or voting rights of the target company. The schedule for the offer is set according to the publication date of the joint prospectus, which is drawn up by the initiator and the target company, or the response note which is drawn up by the target company. Twenty-five listing days separate the date of publication from the closing date and the duration of the offer may not exceed 35 trading days. If the offer is confirmed, giving the initiator two-thirds of the capital and voting rights of target company, the offer reopens for 10 listing days and becomes public within 10 listing days of the publication of the final result. The threshold required for reopening the listing is reduced to a majority of the capital, and voting rights if several offers are present.

The simplified procedure for a public offer can take place if[29]:

– an offer is launched by a shareholder who holds (directly or indirectly) at least half of the capital and voting rights of a company;

28 The time limit begins to run again upon receipt of the required elements.

29 Articles L.233-10, L.225-207 and L.225-209 from the Trade Code.

– an offer is launched by a shareholder who comes to hold (directly or indirectly) after acquisition, at least half of the capital and voting rights of a company;

– an offer is limited to a participation in the capital of the target company. The initiator only targets a participation that is equal to a maximum of 10% of the capital securities which confer voting rights, or 10% of the voting rights of the target company, taking into account similar securities and voting rights they already hold (directly or indirectly);

– an offer is launched by a person to acquire shares with priority dividends, investment certificates or voting right certificates;

– a buyback offer is launched for the shares of a company;

– an offer is issued for which the issuing company proposes the exchange of debt securities which do not give access to capital against equity securities or give access to capital.

The duration of a simplified public offer may be limited to 10 listing days in the presence of a takeover offer and to 15 trading days in other cases, except if it is a buyback offer. The price announced by the initiator may not be lower (unless the AMF advises otherwise) than the price determined by calculating the average share price, weighted by transaction volumes, during the 60 trading days that precede the publication of the notice of filing the proposed public offer. In the case of a public offer for investment certificates or voting rights certificates, the initiator may limit their transaction to the acquisition of a quantity of voting rights certificates or certificates of equal investment rights, or as the case may be, the number of investment certificates or voting rights certificates that they already hold. The price put forward in the context of an offer may be increased, either because of the initiator (overbidding) or because of the launch of a competing offer.

From the opening of an offer and at the latest 5 trading days before its closing date, a proposed competing public offer that targets the securities of the target company, or of one of the target companies, may be filed with the AMF. The initiator may outbid on the terms of the latest competing public offer no later than 5 trading days before closing. A competing public tender offer or a higher bid in cash must be proposed at a price at least 2% higher than the price stipulated above. The initiator may withdraw from their public offer for 5 trading days once the schedule of a competing offer or higher bid has been published. The AMF will then be informed of the decision, which will then be published. The initiator may also withdraw from their offer if, during the offer period, the target company adopts certain implementing measures that modify its nature or if the offer becomes purposeless. When more than 10 weeks have elapsed since the publication of the opening of a public offer, in order to accelerate the comparison of public offers while respecting the alternations, the AMF may set a deadline for the filing of each of the successive overbids. When more than 10 weeks have elapsed since the opening of a public offer, in order to accelerate the outcome of the existing public offers, the AMF may decide to use a last auction system by setting a date for the offers to finally close.

Shleifer and Vishny (1986) propose a model in which three bidders are after the same target: two of them anticipate a high level of synergies, while the third anticipates a significantly lower amount of synergies. According to the two researchers, the value of the target reaches its maximum when the initiator who anticipates the weakest level of synergy is disqualified because of insufficient supply. Thus, their approach underlines that, in certain cases, the target company has an interest in buying back its own shares by proposing a price that includes a premium, in order to eliminate the initiator with whom the synergies implemented would be the weakest. Tietmann (1986) asserts that the target company can profit from the competition between several bidders by announcing to the market that it has provided confidential information to a "white knight" or to a third party likely to launch an offer and with which the level of probable synergies would be greater than that which would be obtained in the context of a merger with one of the other offerors.

The launch of a public offer is mandatory[30] when a physical or legal person holds more than a third of the capital securities or more than a third of the voting rights of a company. It must then inform the AMF and file a draft public offer for all of the capital and securities that give access to the capital or voting rights. This provision also applies when physical or legal persons come to hold, as a result of merger or contributions, more than one-third of the capital securities or voting rights of a company when these securities represent an essential part of the assets of the absorbed or contributed entity. In addition, the launch of a public offer is mandatory when more than a third of the capital or voting rights of a company present on a regulated market is held by another company and constitutes an

30 Article L.233-10 of the Commercial Code (article 356-1-3 of law no. 66-537 from July 24, 1966).

essential part of its assets and no one takes control of the holding company[31]. Finally, the launch of a public offer is mandatory when physical or legal persons, holding a stake of between one-third and one-half of the capital or voting rights of a company, increase the number of equity securities or voting rights they hold by at least 2% in less than 12 consecutive months.

However, cases of where people are exempt from the obligation to launch a public offer can be foreseen. The AMF may authorize the temporary crossing of the threshold of the third party concerned if the overrun relates to less than 3% of the capital and voting rights and if its duration does not exceed 6 months. The persons concerned will not be able to exercise the corresponding voting rights during this period. In addition, it is not mandatory to file a public offer plan when the thresholds referred to above are crossed by a person declaring to act together with one or more shareholders who already hold between one-third and one-half of the capital or rights of company vote. Finally, the AMF may grant an exemption from the obligation to file a proposed public offer if the person or persons concerned can prove that they meet one of the following conditions:

– free transmission between physical persons, distribution of assets carried out by a legal person in proportion to the rights of the partners;

– subscription to the capital increase of a company in a proven situation of financial difficulty, subject to the approval of the general meeting of its shareholders;

– merger or asset contribution transactions, subject to the approval of the general meeting of shareholders;

– combination of a merger or contribution transaction, subject to the approval of the general meeting of shareholders and the conclusion between shareholders of the companies concerned of an agreement constituting a concerted action;

– reduction of the total number of equity securities or of the total number of voting rights that exist in the target company;

– holding of the majority of the company's voting rights by the applicant or by a third party, acting alone or with others;

31 Unless one or several of them already have this control and remain predominant and, in this case, as long as the balance of the respective holdings is not significantly changed.

– reclassification operation, or being analyzed as a reclassification, between companies or persons that belong to the same group.

When the majority shareholder(s) hold(s)[32] at least 95% of the voting rights of a company present on a regulated market or have ceased to be present, a public buyout offer (PBO) may be filed by majority shareholders or required by the AMF, at the request of a holder of securities who confers voting rights, investment certificates or voting rights certificates and who does not belong to the majority group. The PBO is, moreover, compulsory when a public limited company, whose capital securities are admitted on a regulated market, is transformed into a limited partnership with shares. In addition, the initiator of the proposed offer specifies to the AMF whether it reserves the right, at the end of the offer and depending on its outcome, to request that all the equity securities or access to the company's capital and voting rights securities are removed from the regulated market where they are admitted. The public buyout offer is made by purchase on the market at the offer price for a period of at least 10 trading days. However, the company that issues the equity securities and carries out a public buyout offer by exchange may continue to intervene in its own securities as part of the share buyback program[33]. At the end of a PBO, the shareholder or the majority group may see their securities that are not presented by the minority shareholders or the holders of investment certificates or voting rights certificates transferred, if they do not represent any more than 5% of the capital or voting rights, subject to compensation for the latter. When submitting the draft offer, the initiator informs the AMF whether it reserves the right to request that the squeeze-out is implemented once the offer has ended and depending on its outcome, or if they ask that the squeeze-out be carried out as soon as the public buyout offer closes. In support of the proposed offer, the initiator provides the AMF with a valuation of the securities of the target company, carried out according to the objective methods used in the event of the sale of assets, taking into account, according to an appropriate weighting for each case, the value of assets, profits made, market value, existence of subsidiaries and business prospects. If the initiator decides to proceed with the squeeze-out, they inform the AMF of the price offered for the compensation. This price is at least equal to the price of the public buyout offer. It is higher than if the events that are likely

32 Article L.233-10 of the Commercial Code (article 356-1-3 of law no. 66-537 from July 24, 1966).

33 Article L.225-209 of the Commercial Code.

to affect the value of the securities concerned have occurred since the public buyout offer has been admitted. The squeeze-out requires that the securities concerned be unlisted.

1.4.2.2. *Analysis of the financial consequences of an acquisition*

The first constraint that conditions the launch of a public offer is that it creates value for the shareholders of the initiating company. Thus, the accretion rate of earnings per share must first be considered. The transition to IFRS accounting standards, for listed companies that present consolidated accounts, confirms that the linear depreciation of goodwill has disappeared. The second constraint concerns the financing of the operation. It is conditioned by compliance with certain ratios that are examined by banks. These include the debt ratio, debt repayment capacity and financial expense coverage. Finally, to the extent that some of the target's shareholders are legal persons, the initiator must anticipate the analysis of financial consequences, particularly in terms of consolidated income, for the companies invited to sell their shares.

Among the financial consequences of the transaction for the initiator of a public offering, the change in earnings per share (EPS) is presented. This central place in the analysis of the transaction is directly linked to the impact of an increase (or a dilution) of EPS on the market price of the initiator. Indeed, at constant stock market status (thus at constant P/E), any variation in EPS results in a variation of the stock market price in the same proportion. The concern to avoid a decrease in the market capitalization of the initiating company which would make it "OPAble" in turn leads us to consider the EPS accretion rate as one of the main criteria that guides the decision whether or not to complete the transaction. The acquisition leads the initiator to include in its consolidated income group share, a share of the target's net income. The latter corresponds to the percentage of capital acquired at the end of the transaction applied to the consolidated income group share of the target company. The other financial consequences in terms of dilution/relution are different depending on the type of transaction. In a takeover bid, the operation is financed by the net financial debt. This means that the originator goes into debt or uses their available cash, which in both cases results in an increase in net financial debt. In addition, depreciation goodwill and/or valuation difference will reduce the consolidated income group share by as much. The impact of the transaction on consolidated income of the group can be summarized as follows:

Target's share of net income
(Net financial costs from tax generated by the operation) [1.98]
(Depreciation of *goodwill*
And/or the valuation difference)

Impact of the takeover bid on consolidated income shared by the group

Under IFRS, goodwill is not depreciated on a linear basis. However, the impairment test which companies that publish consolidated accounts must perform each year may lead them to write down the net value of goodwill. The EPS relution/dilution rate is equal to:

$$\frac{\text{EPS after} - \text{EPS before}}{\text{EPS before}} = \frac{\text{NR after} - \text{NR before}}{\text{NR before}} \qquad [1.99]$$

where:

– EPS after: EPS of the initiator after the operation;

– EPS before: EPS of the initiator before the operation;

– NR: net result of the company that initiated the operation.

The switch from the formula incorporating EPS to the formula of NRs can be justified by the constancy of the number of shares of the company that initiate the offer at the end of the operation. It is possible to assess the accretive or dilutive nature of the operation before looking at the depreciation of goodwill and/or the valuation difference. Indeed, the takeover bid is accretive if the difference between the share of net income of the QPRN target and the financial expenses net of tax is positive. By dividing each term by the amount of the investment made (in cash), we have:

$$\frac{\text{QPRN}}{\text{I}} - \frac{\text{FF}}{\text{I}} > 0 \text{ so } \frac{\text{QPRN}}{\text{I}} - \text{i} > 0 \text{ or } \frac{\text{QPRN}}{\text{I}} > i \qquad [1.100]$$

where:

– I: investment;

– *i*: cost of debt after tax.

By considering the opposite of each of the unequal terms, we have:

$$\text{P/E target} < \frac{1}{i} \qquad [1.101]$$

By calling the "cash P/E" the $\frac{1}{i}$, ratio, we may deduce that the takeover bid if accretive before taking into account depreciation of goodwill and/or the valuation difference if the P/E of the target is lower than the cash P/E.

In the case of a takeover bid, the operation generally results in a capital increase reserved for shareholders of the target company who agree to contribute their shares to the initiating company. The OPE therefore does not generate any additional net financial costs. However, it results in an increase in the number of shares of the company that initiates the offer, thus creating a dilutive effect.

And so, the impact of the operation on the result consolidated by the group is limited to:

Target's share of net income
(Depreciation of goodwill
and/or the valuation difference) [1.102]

Impact of the OPE on the result consolidated by the group

The EPS relution/dilution rate is given by the formula:

$$\frac{\text{EPS after} - \text{EPS before}}{\text{EPS before}} = \frac{\text{EPS after}}{\text{EPS before}} - 1 \qquad [1.103]$$

It is possible, as in the case of the takeover bid, to determine the accretive or dilutive nature of the operation before taking into account the depreciation of goodwill and/or the valuation difference. The OPE of A on B is accretive if the EPS of A after OPE is greater than the EPS of A before OPE, so:

$$\frac{NR_A + NR_B}{n_A + \frac{P_B}{P_A n_B}} > \frac{NR_A}{n_A} \qquad [1.104]$$

$$\frac{n_A P_A}{NR_A} > \frac{n_B P_B}{NR_B} \frac{P_A}{\frac{NR_A}{n_A}} > \frac{P_B}{\frac{NR_B}{n_B}} \qquad [1.105]$$

$$\frac{P_A}{EPS_A} > \frac{P_B}{EPS_B} \qquad [1.106]$$

where:

– NR_A: net result of the initiating company A;

– RN_B: net result of the target company B;

– n_A: number of shares in the capital of A before OPE;

– n_B: number of shares in the capital of B before OPE;

– P_A: price of A;

– P_B: price of B.

Finally, the takeover bid is accretive before taking into account the provisions for goodwill depreciation and/or the valuation difference if the P/E of the initiator is greater than the P/E of the target company. In the case of a direct merger, the operation is based on exchange parity and results in an increase in the capital of the acquiring company. However, such a transaction does not generate goodwill. Also, the impact of the operation on the net income group share of the acquiring company, which determines its rate of increase in EPS, is limited to the share of the net income of the absorbed company, which is apprehended following the merger-absorption. Hansen (1985) points out that takeover by way of a public exchange offer allows the shareholders of the target company to benefit from a part of the gains anticipated by the initiator of the operation.

The synergies correspond to the pre-tax surplus earnings that the companies that merge together could not have achieved in isolation. The first category of synergies relates to the costs linked to getting rid of the head office of one of the two companies, along with workforce reductions and improving supply conditions. The second category concerns development synergies, i.e. obtaining of new commercial outlets for the complementary products of the companies that come together. When examining merger events, Mandelker (1974) finds that the value created through synergies benefits the shareholders of the acquired company. This conclusion results from abnormal returns on the shares of the acquired companies, while the shares of the companies initiating the mergers show no significant gain or loss of return. Therefore, synergies represent the externalization of a gain that the shareholders of the acquired company realize only on the day of the merger. However, this potential should be detected and properly valued before the merger takes place in an efficient market. Ellert (1976) explains this by asserting that the management of acquired firms is inefficient, and that mergers turn out to be the best way to allow the market to play its role in optimizing the allocation of firm resources.

The debt ratio or gearing ratio – which corresponds to the ratio between consolidated net financial debt and consolidated shareholders' equity – is also a criterion for investment decisions. A debt ratio greater than 1 is deemed unacceptable and results in a downgrade of the company's financial rating by specialist agencies (Moody's, Standard & Poor's, Fitch IBCA, etc.), as well as an increase in the cost of the debt. This situation therefore implies a strategic refocusing of the group leading it to pursue a divestment policy, with the aim of restoring its financial structure. The takeover bid leads to an increase in net financial debt due to the debt generated by the operation. Equity increases by the amount of minority interests (those shown on the target's balance sheet and those generated by the operation). They then correspond to the share of the net equity of the target that is not held by the initiator at the end of the takeover operation, given an offer's success rate of less than 100%. The OPE does not generate increased debt to finance the operation. Equity, for its part, appreciates up to the minority interests that appear on the target's balance sheet and due to the capital increase, including premium, that is generated by the operation. In the event of a direct merger, the impact on the debt ratio is almost identical to that of a public exchange offer:

– increase in the net financial debt of the acquiring company by the amount of net debt of the absorbed company, if the latter is not fully consolidated before the merger-absorption;

– increase in shareholders' equity by recovering minority interests in the absorbed company (if the latter is not fully consolidated before the operation) and by the capital increase, including premium, generated by the operation.

Two ratios are considered by banks and analysts to be significant of the debt repayment capacity:

– the ratio between the consolidated net financial debt and the consolidated self-financing capacity (SFC)[34] must be less than 3;

– the ratio between the consolidated net financial debt and the consolidated EBIDTA must be less than 4.

The takeover bid, financed by an increase in net financial debt, results in a reduction in financial income and a change in corporation tax due to the tax deductibility of interest charges. In addition, if the initiator does not consolidate the target before the full consolidation transaction, its consolidated cash flow and consolidated EBITDA are, respectively, increased by those of the target. The OPE does not generate additional financial costs. Consequently, the consolidated CAF and EBITDA are only increased by those of the target, if the latter is not fully consolidated before the operation. The impacts of the direct merger on CAF and EBITDA are identical to those of a takeover bid: respective recovery of the CAF of the absorbed company and its EBITDA insofar as the latter is not fully consolidated before the merger-absorption.

The financial expense coverage ratio, which must be greater than 4, is the ratio between consolidated feedback and consolidated financial expense net of financial income. If the target company is not fully consolidated before the offer (or the merger), the operating profit and the net financial expenses of the initiating company increase, respectively, from those of the target at the end of the transaction. In the case of a takeover bid, the financial expenses increase by the amount of the acquisition debt.

Following a takeover bid, the company that contributed the shares of the target company it held to the offer will show exceptional income in its consolidated accounts. This result relates to the difference between their sale price and their cost price on the consolidated balance sheet. The latter corresponds to the share of equity held by the transferor and possibly revalued after the acquisition of securities. In addition, the goodwill disappears from the transferor's balance sheet through a depreciation item,

34 The SFC corresponds to the difference between the products that are cashable/collected and the disbursable/disbursed charges. It can be calculated using net income by neutralizing accounting aggregates that impacted the net income without having an impact on cash flow (depreciation, amortization and provisions, book value of assets sold in terms of non-disbursable charges and reversals of depreciation and provisions, share of subsidies transferred to the income statement in terms of non-cashable income).

insofar as its value corresponds to the estimate of future profits that the transferred company was expected to provide to the transferor. Finally, the potential payment of tax on the capital gain within the sale by the transferor reduces its consolidated income (group share) by the same amount. In total, the impact of a sale on the consolidated income of a group corresponds to:

Consolidated capital gain or loss
(Depreciation of net *goodwill*)
(Capital gains tax) [1.107]

Impact on the consolidated income of group share

At the end of a takeover bid, the transferor renounces their share in the future results of the target company. However, they save financial charges on their acquisition debt, which they can repay. In addition, they may place an amount of their capital gain on sale on the market. Considering that the placement rate and the borrowing rate are close, the sale results in a loss of a share of net income and in a loss of financial income, calculated on the basis of the sale amount.

1.4.2.3. *Share buybacks*

The PSBO (public share buyback offer) may target any percentage of the capital provided that the company has a sufficient amount of distributable reserves[35]. The PSBO is a public offer under a simplified procedure. The company must justify the offer price in a note approved by the AMF through a multi-criteria analysis. The capital gain generated by shareholders who follow the offer is treated for tax purposes as a dividend, not giving rise to the right to tax credit.

The PSBP (personal share buyback program) gives rise to the publication of an information document not approved by the AMF. This document specifies:

– the objectives of the program;

– the legal framework of the operation (text of the draft resolution of the general assembly);

35 All reserves are distributable with the exception of the legal reserve and revaluation reserve.

– the terms of the operation:

- percentage of the target capital capped at 10% after deduction of shares already held by the company,

- duration and timing of the operation. The period is capped at 18 months from the date of the general meeting called to rule on the operation,

- financing of the operation corresponding to self-financing or debt;

– elements that make it possible to assess the financial impact of the operation in terms of:

- debt ratio: net financial debt is increased by the amount of the repurchase and shareholders' equity is reduced by the same amount (when the repurchased securities will be canceled),

- EPS before and after taking into account dilutive securities. The net result is reduced by financial expenses (net of IS) generated by the increase in net financial debt. The number of shares is reduced by the number of shares canceled at the end of the transaction;

– the tax consequences of the operation:

- for the company initiating the transaction, there is no tax impact if the repurchased securities are subsequently canceled. If the securities are not intended to be canceled but sold or transferred at a price different from that of their repurchase, the operation will have an impact on taxable income,

- for the transferor, the capital gain is taxed for individuals and companies if the securities are resold less than 2 years after their acquisition. If the securities sold within the framework of the buyback offer have been held for more than 2 years, only 5% of the capital gain is reintegrated into tax income for the share of costs and charges;

– the intentions of the persons controlling the initiator alone or with others with regard to the sale of securities as part of the transaction;

– recent significant events relating to the company since the last publication of its information (annual report, information note relating to a financial operation, etc.);

– the person responsible for the information note, usually the CEO of the initiating company.

Therefore, if a company intends to buy back up to 10% of its capital, it chooses the method of the operation according to its “tax customers”:

– if the shareholders are mainly individuals, the PRAP is chosen;

– if the shareholders are companies that are eligible for the “parent-subsidiary” scheme, the OPRA is chosen;

– if the shareholders are companies which have held the securities for more than 2 years (and their participation is insufficient to allow them to benefit from the “parent-subsidiary” scheme), the company will choose the PRAP.

In the context of an acquisition of a listed target by takeover or takeover bid, valuation by traditional approaches favor negotiations between buyer and seller. When a shareholder wishes to withdraw from the capital of a company, they undertake negotiations with another company through an advisory bank. The acquirer who takes control of the target and integrates it into their overall strategy must agree to pay a control premium[36]. The transferor can use investment funds that take control of the target company via a takeover holding company. The value of the target is then no longer to be assumed but is proven: it represents the maximum amount of funds that can be raised by the takeover holding company in the form of capital, subscribed by the investment and debt fund(s). Determining the value of the target company means structuring how the holding company is financed.

An LBO (leverage buy out) is the purchase of a company financed by debt through a buyout fund that involves the managers of the company from a financial point of view. What is more, the goal of the buyout is not only to obtain an enhanced level of profitability by playing on the leverage effect, as no value is created. The buyout’s success is mainly explained through an increase in motivation of the leaders who are more invested in the success of the company. A better allocation of resources in favor of the shareholders will be achieved. The key interests of managers are therefore twofold: a financial interest relating to their immediate or potential participation (stock options) in the capital, and a desire to maintain their jobs and their reputation by ensuring that the company does not go bankrupt. Highly profitable and without much investment potential, mature companies are the perfect candidates for buyouts. Jensen (1989) demonstrates that in the absence of

36 If the target’s attractiveness is strong and/or if the competition with other prospective buyers is significant, they may agree to pay part of the valuation of the anticipated synergies.

heavy debt, the natural temptation of managers is to use their significant free cash flow to increase their size, to the detriment of their profitability, by overinvesting or by diversifying out of their business verticals. This most often leads to the destruction of value. The only value creation enabled by debt lies in the significant demand it places on managers to better manage economic assets.

1.4.3. *Leveraged buyout operations*

A leveraged buyout operation or LBO consists of acquiring a target company by an *ad hoc* takeover holding company which is financed to a large extent by debt. The acquisition of the holding's equity solely by investors results in a down payment that is less than that which would be necessary to purchase the target's shares, thus taking full advantage of the leverage effect (financial profitability of the target company above the cost of the debt).

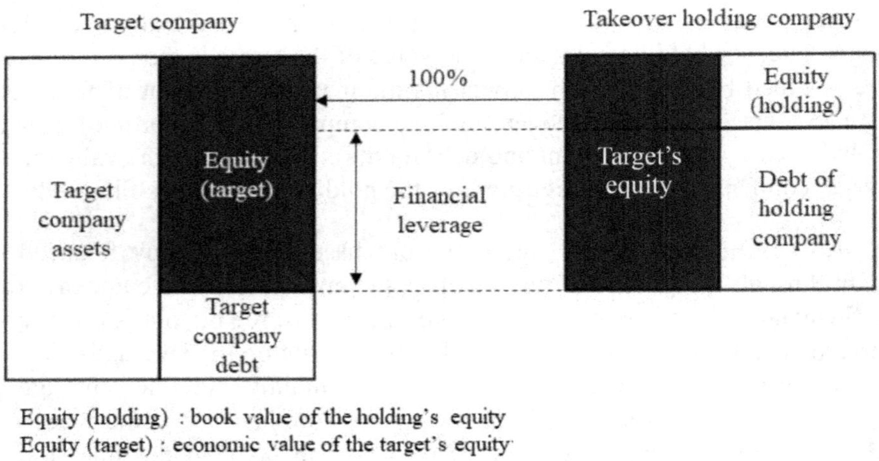

Figure 1.5. *Principle of a leverage operation*

The holding's acquisition debt is reimbursed by the dividends paid by the target and potentially by the cash provided by the exit from the LBO. This is the reason why the latter assumes certain conditions previously met to ensure the viability of the framework and to generate an acceptable level of risk. Also, the target must exercise their activity in a mature sector that requires moderate investments and holds low debt, in order to promote the distribution of high dividends to the takeover holding company. Environmental threats must be limited in order to reduce the risks that relate to the realization of the business plan in terms of competitive intensity, risk of calling into question the position of the target due to technological innovation and to cyclicality of activity.

The target company must also have a reliable and realistic business plan on which the financial simulations are based. It is important to have good visibility on the exit by IPO or by sale to an industry player or to another fund. We may frequently observe the transferor reinvesting in the capital of the takeover holding company. This reinvestment then secures the investment of the new fund, insofar as it constitutes a pledge to keep the current management in place, and gives credibility to the business plan relating to it. The conditions for a transferred reinvestment are the same as those of the emergence of the new fund. Reinvestment is also advantageous for the transferor because by carrying out such an operation, they are then about to mobilize only part of the cash received. In addition, they will benefit from the same IRR as the new fund as well as an upside potential when it exits the LBO, and thus will be able to benefit from certain tax advantages.

The target sale price is capped up to the maximum amount of funds likely to be raised by the buyout holding company. The amount of acquisition debt is directly linked to the expected profitability of the target company. The amount is calibrated according to several constraints. The first is to integrate a repayment over a period of 7–9 years, using the dividends distributed by the target to the holding company (assuming that the profit distribution rate of the target is at 100% from the start of the LBO). The second is to calibrate the operation so that the holding company retains slightly excess cash flow, so as not to generate additional financing needs. The third is to comply with certain financial ratios (covenants) which allow lending institutions and financiers to effectively control the smooth running of the LBO. Equity is set at a level that ensures that investors (and investment funds) receive an internal rate of return (IRR) of around 20–30% in 3 years, in the event of an exit from the fund by IPO or by transfer to a manufacturer or another fund on the basis of a multiple of gross operating surplus or operating profit. The target value is actually slightly less than the sum of the values of equity and of the debt of the holding company. Indeed, the latter must also finance various costs relating to the acquisition (of around 3–4% of the transaction value). These expenses generally correspond to the costs of hiring lawyers, getting advice, legal, accounting and tax audits and the payment of a commitment fee on the acquisition debt.

Optimizing the holding's finances during the first years of the LBO will mean that part of the repayment of the acquisition debt is deferred. This senior debt is broken down into two parts. The first, called part A (80% of the total amount), is repayable by capital depreciation, and increases slightly over 7 years. The interest is calculated on the basis of the 6-month Euribor rate plus basis points. The second, called part B (20% of the total amount), is repayable at the end of 8 years and bears interest at the 6-month Euribor rate, also increasing from the basis point. The financing can be supplemented by a mezzanine debt, generally repayable after 9 years, or at 50% after 8 years and 50% after 9 years. Here, interest is calculated on the basis of the 6-month Euribor plus basis points to which the capitalized basis points are added. This mezzanine debt is accompanied by stock subscription warrants (SSW), which generate a capital gain that improves the performance of mezzanine financing providers (often referred to as "mezzaners").

In the event that the holding's cash flow is in deficit the first year, it is possible to envisage payment of an exceptional dividend by the target to the holding (with the condition of having distributable reserves), or the negotiation with banks of an "overfinancing" of the holding company, i.e. an increase in acquisition debt making it possible to cover cash requirements during the year. Kaplan (1989) and Smith (1990) show in particular that, over the period 1980–1985, the LBO improved the efficiency and performance of the acquired company.

The reduction in the tax payable by the group, made up of the holding company and the target, optimizes the operation thanks to tax integration. The tax group can use the tax deficit created by financial charges and the depreciation of acquisition costs of the holding company when the latter does not have taxable income (dividends go up tax-free within the scope of integration tax). The taxable results of the target are thus partially neutralized by the holding's deficit for tax purposes. Thus, the target pays the holding company the corporate tax (IS) that it would have paid to the public treasury, in the absence of fiscal integration. The tax is liquidated vis-à-vis the holding company according to the principle of installments. In other words, during year N, down payments on corporate tax are paid for the current year and the liquidation balance[37] is adjusted during the following year. In addition, the holding company pays the tax, the base of which corresponds to the taxable result of the target, reduced by the holding's tax deficit. The conditions for reinvesting target shareholders in the capital of the takeover holding company can be optimized. The first axis concerns the contribution of part of the shares of the target to the takeover holding company. In this case, the capital gain on the disposal generated by the contributor is tax deferred until the date of disposal of the securities of the holding company which paid for the contribution. The second axis concerns the transfer of securities within the tax consolidation scope of the transferor. In this case, the takeover holding company must be part of the tax consolidation scope of the transferor before the LBO, and the entry of equity investors must be temporarily limited to less than 5%. This then assumes that 95% of the fund's investment lies in the acquisition of bonds convertible into shares, or bonds redeemable into shares. Thus, the capital gain is unrealized. The third axis is around the reinvestment of the transferor as a physical person, in the amount of more than 25% of the capital of the holding company. In this case, the reinvestment amount is deductible from the ISF, and the shares held are assimilated to a work tool.

Distributing all of the target's income to the holding company (achieved during the previous financial year) leads to recalculating the financial debt and the target's financial income. Beyond the business plan period, forecasts can be extended over 9 years using the following assumptions:

– activity growth rate equal to that expected for the last year of the business plan, or linear convergence (linear interpolation) towards a more normative activity growth rate (somewhere between 2 and 3%);

– main ratios observed in the last year of the business plan maintained beyond:

- EBIDTA or EBIT margin rate,

- ratio: depreciation expense/turnover,

- ratio: investments/revenue. The level of investments must, however, be in relation to the observed growth if this is variable,

- ratio: net working capital/revenue.

37 Difference between IS actually due and the sum of installments already paid.

In the absence of additional information, minority interests and the projections for risks and charges in the opening balance sheet are assumed to be constant over the entire period selected for the LBO. The construction of the target's balance sheet is based on forecasted cash flows which make it possible to determine the net financial debt.

Net result of the target N	
+ Depreciation and amortization N	
(Net investments of disposals N)	[1.108]
(Variation in net working capital N)	
(Dividend paid for the year N-1)	
Variation in net debt of the target N, assimilated to cash flow	

The balance sheet at 31/12/N is obtained from that at 31/12/N-1:

Fixed assets N	=	Fixed Assets (N-1) + Investments N – Allocations N	
Net working capital N	=	Net working capital (N-1) + Variation of net working capital	[1.109]
Total asset N	=	Total asset (N-1) + Investment N – Allocations N + Variation of net working capital N	

Equity N	=		
Provisions N	=	Equity (N-1) + Result N – Dividends	
Net debt N	=	Provisions (N-1)	
		Net debt (N-1) – Cash-flow N	[1.110]
Total liabilities N	=	Total liability (N-1) + Result N – Dividends – *Cash-flow* N	

This presentation makes it possible to demonstrate, by recurrence, the balance sheet balance at 12/31/N, under the assumption of a balance sheet balanced at 12/31/N-1, by replacing cash flow by its value:

Liability N = Liability (N-1) + Result N – Dividends
– (Result N + Allocations N – Investments N [1.111]
– Variations in net working capital N – Dividends)

By simplifying by result N and Dividends N and by considering the fact that the liability (N-1) is equal to the asset (N-1), we therefore have:

Liability N = Asset (N-1) – Allocations N + Investments N
+ Variations in net working capital N [1.112]
= Total asset N

In addition, the maximum debt of the holding company must be set at a level such that the cash flow always remains positive. The net result of the holding company on which the determination of its cash flow is based supposes the preliminary calculation of the tax due, under the tax consolidation agreement. The tax paid by the integrated tax group is determined on the basis of the taxable result of the target, assimilated to its current result before taxes (CRBT) from which the depreciation and amortization of acquisition costs are deducted, on the one hand, and, on the other hand, the financial expenses on the acquisition debt, to which the financial income generated by the investment of the takeover holding company are added where applicable.

And so:

CRBT of the target
(Depreciation of the acquisition costs of the holding company)
(Financial costs on acquisition debt) [1.113]
+ Financial income on the investment of the holding company's cash
Taxable result of the tax group

The holding's net income includes dividends received from the target, tax received from the target, depreciation and amortization of acquisition costs, financial costs generated by the acquisition debt and the balance of tax payable to the public treasury.

And so:

Dividends received from the target (N-1)
+ Tax received from the target
(Depreciation of acquisition costs)
(Financial charges on acquisition debt) [1.114]
+ Financial income on the investment of the holding company's cash
(IS transferred to the public treasury)
Net result of the holding

The holding company's balance sheet is based on its cash flow, determined from net income and the repayment schedule of the acquisition debt. The cash flow of the holding company is determined from its net income. It is then necessary to reinstate the amortization of acquisition costs, and to deduct the amount to be repaid from the acquisition debt.

And so:

Net result of the holding
+ Depreciation of acquisition costs
(Repayment of the principal of the acquisition debt) [1.115]
Cash flow of the holding company

Senior acquisition debt is repaid by constant amortization or, in a more aggressive case, by progressive amortization.

The holding company balance sheet then shows the cash flow to be maintained at a positive level:

Securities N	=	Securities (N-1)	
Acquisition costs N	=	Acquisition costs (N-1) – Allocations N	
Treasury N	=	Treasury (N-1) + *Cash-flow* N	[1.116]
Total asset N	=	Total asset (N-1) + *Cash-flow* N – Allocations N	
Equity N	=	Equity (N-1) + Result N	
Financial debt N	=	Financial debt (N-1) – Debt repayment N	[1.117]
Total liability N	=	Total liability (N-1) + Net result N – Debt repayment N	

Replacing cash flow N by its value makes it possible to establish, by recurrence, like for the target, the balance of the holding company balance sheet.

The maximum amount of the holding's equity must be set at a level such that the IRR of equity investors reaches the desired level (around 30% in 3 years).

It is determined by successive iterations by simulating different levels of debt. The IRR of equity investors is determined by comparing the valuation of the group (holding and target) at the time of their exit from the holding's capital, with the valuation retained for the target at the time of their entry:

– V_n: equity value of the set made up of the holding company and the target in *n* years; in other words, V_n is the exit value of equity investors (private equity funds);

– V: amount of fund investment;

– *i*: IRR required by the fund.

During the entire investment period, the fund does not receive dividends, so as to optimize the service of the acquisition debt. Therefore, we find:

$$V = \frac{0}{1+i} + \frac{0}{(1+i)^2} + \cdots + \frac{V_n}{(1+i)^n} \qquad [1.118]$$

V is the present value at the required IRR of the output value. The group's V_n value (holding and target) that results from stock market comparisons (application of a multiple of EBIT or EBITDA) includes its net financial debt, from the consolidated balance sheet.

Consolidated opening balance sheet at 31/12/N	**Consolidated closing balance sheet at 31/12/N+1**
Target fixed assets N Target working capital N Holding costs N Goodwill N	Target fixed assets N+1 Target working capital N+1 Holding costs N+1 Goodwill N
Total consolidated asset N	Total consolidated asset N+1
Holding equity N Consolidated reserves N Target net debt N Holding net debt N	Holding equity N+1 Consolidated reserves N + target result N+1 Target net debt N+1 Holding net debt N+1
Total consolidated liability N	Total consolidated liability N+1

Table 1.12. *Consolidated opening and closing balance sheets of the holding company*

By way of illustration, an LBO was carried out on the Carrefour SA company. Based on the forecasts from zonebourse.com analysts, the income statement is extended according to the same logic as that which underlies the valuation by the DCF method:

– linear convergence of the activity growth rate from 5.4% in 2016 (last year of financial analyst forecasts) to 3% in 2021;

– maintenance from 2016 of the following ratios observed:

- operational margin of 5.4%,

- ratio reporting depreciation and amortization to turnover at 1.9%;

– cost of debt at 3.5% from 2017;

– IS rate at 38%.

The change in net financial debt from the last published balance sheet (2013) is based on forecast cash flows. These include:

– dividends as part of a distribution rate of 100% in order to optimize the service of the holding company's acquisition debt;

– investments which converge linearly between 2017 and 2021 towards the amount of depreciation allowances for the last year;

– the change in WCR determined from the WCR/turnover ratio (-7.7%) assumed to be constant within the business plan.

Carrefour target income statement (€ million)	Production	Source zonebourse.com			Extension				
	2013	2014	2015	2016	2017	2018	2019	2020	2021
Turnover	74,888	75,384	78,760	81,672	84,578	87,469	90,337	93,173	95,968
Growth rate		0.7%	4.5%	3.7%	3.6%	3.4%	3.3%	3.1%	3.0%
EBITDA	3,669	3,840	4,125	4,421	4,578	4,735	4,890	5,044	5,195
EBITDA margin rate	4.9%	5.1%	5.2%	5.4%	5.4%	5.4%	5.4%	5.4%	5.4%
(Allocations)	(1,432)	(1,413)	(1,511)	(1,572)	(1,628)	(1,684)	(1,739)	(1,793)	(1,847)
Allocations/turnover	-1.9%	-1.9%	-1.9%	-1.9%	-1.9%	-1.9%	-1.9%	-1.9%	-1.9%
EBIT	2,237	2,427	2,614	2,849	2,950	3,051	3,151	3,250	3,348
(Net financial costs)	(578)	(521)	(541)	(515)	(203)	(210)	(215)	(214)	(207)
Cost of debt					3.5%	3.5%	3.5%	3.5%	3.5%
RIBT	1,659	1,906	2,073	2,334	2,747	2,841	2,936	3,036	3,140
(IS)	(631)	(724)	(788)	(887)	(1,044)	(1,079)	(1,116)	(1,154)	(1,193)
IS rate		38.0%	38.0%	38.0%	38.0%	38.0%	38.0%	38.0%	38.0%
Net result	*1,028*	*1,182*	*1,285*	*1,447*	*1,703*	*1,761*	*1,820*	*1,882*	*1,947*

Table 1.13. *Forecast of activity and operational profitability of the Carrefour SA*

Cash flow of target Carrefour (millions €)	Production	Prolongation							
	2013	2014	2015	2016	2017	2018	2019	2020	2021
Net income	1,028	1,182	1,285	1,447	1,703	1,761	1,820	1,882	1,947
(Dividend)		(1,028)	(1,182)	(1,285)	(1,447)	(1,703)	(1,761)	(1,820)	(1,882)
Depreciations & Amortizations		1,413	1,511	1,572	1,628	1,684	1,739	1,793	1,847
(Investments)		(2,311)	(2,302)	(2,416)	(2,302)	(2,188)	(2,075)	(1,961)	(1,847)
(ΔWCR)		38	260	225	224	223	221	219	216
Cash flow = Net debt		(706)	(427)	(458)	(194)	(224)	(56)	113	280

Table 1.14. *Cash flow forecast for the Carrefour SA target*

Simplified financial statement of the target Carrefour (millions €)	Production	Extension							
	2013	2014	2015	2016	2017	2018	2019	2020	2021
Assets	22,107	23,005	23,796	24,640	25,314	25,819	26,155	26,323	26,323
WCR	(5,775)	(5,813)	(6,074)	(6,298)	(6,522)	(6,745)	(6,966)	(7,185)	(7,401)
Total asset	16,332	17,192	17,722	18,342	18,792	19,074	19,189	19,138	18,922
Equity	8,597	8,751	8,854	9,016	9,272	9,330	9,389	9,451	9,516
Provisions	3,618	3,618	3,618	3,618	3,618	3,618	3,618	3,618	3,618
Net debt	4,117	4,823	5,250	5,708	5,902	6,126	6,182	6,068	5,788
Equity & liabilities	16,332	17,192	17,722	18,342	18,792	19,074	19,189	19,138	18,922
WCR/CA	-7.7 %	-7.7 %	-7.7 %	-7.7 %	-7.7 %	-7.7 %	-7.7 %	-7.7 %	-7.7 %

Table 1.15. *Provisional assessment of the Carrefour SA target*

Holding's debt due date (millions €)	Production	Extension							
	2013	2014	2015	2016	2017	2018	2019	2020	2021
Amount left to pay	6,900	6,038	5,175	4,313	3,450	2,588	1,725	863	0
(Amortization of principal)		(863)	(863)	(863)	(863)	(863)	(863)	(863)	(863)
In % of nominal		12.50%	12.50%	12.50%	12.50%	12.50%	12.50%	12.50%	12.50%
Euribor 6 M		0.18%	0.18%	0.18%	0.18%	0.18%	0.18%	0.18%	0.18%
Margin on Euribor (*spread*)		2.75%	2.75%	2.75%	2.75%	2.75%	2.75%	2.75%	2.75%
Cost of SWAP		1.00%	1.00%	1.00%	1.00%	1.00%	1.00%	1.00%	1.00%
Cost of debt		3.93%	3.93%	3.93%	3.93%	3.93%	3.93%	3.93%	3.93%
Average debt		6,469	5,606	4,744	3,881	3,019	2,156	1,294	431
Financial costs		254	220	186	153	119	85	51	17

Table 1.16. *Holding's debt schedule*

Holding's income statement (millions €)	Production	Prolongation							
	2013	2014	2015	2016	2017	2018	2019	2020	2021
Dividends received from the target		1,028	1,182	1,285	1,447	1,703	1,761	1,820	1,882
(Financial costs)		(254)	(220)	(186)	(153)	(119)	(85)	(51)	(17)
Tax received from the target		724	788	887	1,044	1,079	1,116	1,154	1,193
(Tax to pay to the public treasury)		(628)	(704)	(816)	(986)	(1,034)	(1,083)	(1,134)	(1,187)
Net income		870	1,045	1,170	1,353	1,630	1,709	1,789	1,872

Tax group	Production	Prolongation							
	2013	2014	2015	2016	2017	2018	2019	2020	2021
Target's income before tax		1,906	2,073	2,334	2,747	2,841	2,936	3,036	3,140
(Financial costs of H)		(254)	(220)	(186)	(153)	(119)	(85)	(51)	(17)
Income of tax group		1,652	1,853	2,148	2,595	2,722	2,851	2,985	3,123
(Tax to pay to the public treasury)		(628)	(704)	(816)	(986)	(1,034)	(1,083)	(1,134)	(1,187)

Holding's cash flows (millions €)	Production	Prolongation							
	2013	2014	2015	2016	2017	2018	2019	2020	2021
Net income		870	1,045	1,170	1,353	1,630	1,709	1,789	1,872
(Amortization of the principal)		(863)	(863)	(863)	(863)	(863)	(863)	(863)	(863)
***Cash flow* = D Treasury**		8	183	307	490	767	846	926	1,009

Balance sheet of the holding	Production	Prolongation							
	2013	2014	2015	2016	2017	2018	2019	2020	2021
Shares of the target	16,641	16,641	16,641	16,641	16,641	16,641	16,641	16,641	16,641
Treasury	0	8	191	498	988	1,755	2,601	3,527	4,537
Total asset	16,641	16,648	16,831	17,138	17,628	18,395	19,242	20,168	21,177
Equity	9,741	10,611	11,656	12,826	14,178	15,808	17,517	19,305	21,177
Acquisition debt	6,900	6,038	5,175	4,313	3,450	2,588	1,725	863	0
Equity & liabilities	16,641	16,648	16,831	17,138	17,628	18,395	19,242	20,168	21,177

Table 1.17. *Provisional accounts of the holding company of the Carrefour SA target*

Determining the acquisition debt falls within the following framework:

– linear amortization over 8 years;

– cost of debt from the 6-month Euribor which includes a hedging cost (1%) and a margin (2.75%);

– amount set in such a way that the holding company cash flow is always positive.

The amount of the holding's equity (€9.7 billion) is determined so that the 3-year internal rate of return (IRR) for investors (private equity funds) is 20% (Table 1.18).

Determination of the holding's capital	**Production**	**Prolongation**		
	2013	**2014**	**2015**	**2016**
Market capitalization of the target	16,576			
Net debt	4,117			
Entreprise value	20,693			
EBIT	2,237			
Multiple of Ebit	*9.3*			*9.3*
EBIT				2,849
Enterprise exit value				26,354
Net debt of the target				5,708
Acquisition debt of H (rest to pay)				4,313
(H treasury)				(498)
Consolidated net debt exit from target				9,523
Economic value of exit equity				16,832
IRR required by the investment fund				20%
Entry capital of the takeover holding company	*9,741*			

Table 1.18. *Determination of the capital amount of the takeover holding company*

Consequently, in the event of an LBO, Carrefour SA would be valued at €16.8 billion, or 1.5% more than its market capitalization.

1.5. Conclusion

The market value of economic assets is divided between the economic value of equity and net debt. According to the theory of equilibrium markets, there exists an optimal financial structure that would be linked to the tax savings due to the tax deductibility of interest charges. However, taking into account personal taxes, bankruptcy and restructuring costs call into question the validity of this reasoning, as it goes against the tax advantage of debt at the corporate level. Indeed, the value of an indebted business can be greater than that of a non-indebted business. The optimal debt ratio would be achieved when the present value of the tax savings, which results from additional debt, is simply offset by the increase in the present value of the costs of dysfunction and bankruptcy that this entails[38]. Moreover, integrating investor taxation turns out to be another constraint on this reasoning. Indeed, in practice, income from equity is taxed less than the income from debt, insofar as the tax advantage of debt for a company is lessened by the tax advantage of equity. In addition, in recent years, state tax reforms have tended to eliminate the corporate debt tax advantage[39]. Moreover, the theory of equilibrium markets considers the company to be a single actor. However, in practice, theories coming from organizations seem to reflect reality to a higher degree. Indeed, the decision to take out debt for a company is above all the result of agency conflicts between the various stakeholders of the company or of a desire to send a signal to the market that it is only a study of the structure and the cost (within the limit of debt ratios). Valuation methods estimate enterprise value in order to derive the economic value of equity. The three traditional methods based on wealth, stock market considerations and business plans are supposed to be combined to find the most accurate value. This exercise is particularly useful in the corporate control market. It helps guide the shareholders and orient the strategy to be implemented.

Depending on the contexts of specific financial structures, or on the company's position in its life cycle, the literature on traditional valuation methods advocates for the use of some methods over others. These recommendations are derived from empirical results for which the authors first make theoretical adjustments. This means optimizing and making the application of these results more reliable in order to reach a fair value.

---

38 As the debt increases, the enterprise value is negatively impacted as the indebted company can no longer make a profit and therefore take advantage of the tax benefit. If the situation persists, the company finds itself in a difficult situation and is forced to incur bankruptcy costs (severance payments, legal costs). In addition, an indebted company must incur restructuring costs to meet its debt repayment deadlines and may lose profitable investment opportunities because it can no longer finance itself. These dysfunction costs correspond to reductions in research and development or training costs.

39 In France, since 2014, only 75% of interest is tax deductible.

2

The Performance of the Assessment and the Creation of Value from Control Operations

2.1. Introduction

Theoretical adjustments aim first of all to reconcile the traditional view of the optimal financial structure with the Modigliani–Miller theorem. To do this, Farrar and Selwyn (1967), Brennan (1970) and Dickinson and Kyuno (1977) find that the integration of the taxation of individuals and their aversion to risk are key factors in determining the choice of additional debt for the company. Then, due to the simplicity of its implementation, the capital cash flow method of Ruback (1998) can prove to be an alternative approach to the DCF method without needing to change the valuation result. In addition, the concept of duration discussed by Arnold and North (2008) may be important to make the hypothetical parameters reliable when building a business plan through the DCF method. Finally, Shaffer (2006) attempts to integrate the risk of bankruptcy into the DCF method.

While from a theoretical standpoint, the discounted cash flow method seems to be the most reliable insofar as it takes into account a potential change in discounted cash flows at a rate that corresponds to the cost of capital, empirically, the preference of one valuation method over another depends on a variety of factors. In reality, according to Kaplan and Ruback (1995), if we are talking about leveraged buyout operations, the methods that adopt business plans actually prove to be more suitable than the approaches based on multiples. However, Alford (1992) asserts that the P/E ratio is more precise once an appropriate benchmark has been established. The sample should ideally include companies in the same industry with similar financial structures and portfolio value of assets. In the same way, according to Damodaran (2009), the valuation of a young company (whose cash flow forecasting is more than delicate, or at least, it must be carried out in the short term) seems to be able to be carried out from sales or net income, discounted at a target rate of return. Moreover, by focusing on specific contexts such as the takeover of companies that have gone bankrupt, Hotchkiss and Mooradian (1998) find that the prices paid are initially based on a valuation that results from the multiple of turnover or assets. However, given the large disparities between the prices paid and the initial valuations that emerge within such contexts, it seems that company valuation that relates to the negotiation margin of the different stakeholders is, in this context, more of an exercise used for strategic purposes than a purely financial tool aimed at uncovering real value. According to Gilson *et al.* (2000), these disparities are not the result of calculation errors but rather resulting from deficiencies in the quality of information and conflicts between agencies.

The valuation of a company is used in particular to estimate the value of its buyout so that the synergies that result from the transaction can create value. It therefore seems interesting to know whether empirically such situations prove to be true. When buying out companies that are bankrupt, Hotchkiss and Mooradian (1998) estimate that only the target company sees its share price increase in the days that follow the transaction. More generally, the study by Moeller *et al.* (2004) concludes that taking control of a company does not create value. Thus, the interest in conducting such operations is more linked to the reasons for expanding the group's influence on the market, and is justified in terms of remuneration beyond simple errors of assessment, which are consequences of the unfounded optimism from business leaders.

2.2. Theoretical adjustments

In order to reconcile the traditional view of optimizing financial structures with the Modigliani–Miller theorem, Dickinson and Kyuno (1977) constitute a model in which they incorporate the tax on capital gains, dividends and interest earned. They believe that investors arbitrate their decision to participate according to the possible benefit of personal leverage.

They note that if the market is dominated by aggressive investors who demonstrate significant risk aversion, the company would do well to go into debt. Conversely, if the market is dominated by cautious investors, additional debt would lessen the corporate tax advantage. Farrar and Selwyn (1967) assess corporate financial policies with respect to income after-tax that is received by an investor. Their study points to the affirmation that the policy of the financial structure depends on the marginal tax rates of investors and the policy of paying dividends. For his part, Brennan (1970) shows that the implementation of a leverage strategy that maximizes enterprise value turns out to be attractive to all investors, provided that the corporate tax rate is higher than the effective tax rate in the market.

Regarding the theoretical adjustments to the method of discounting cash flows, Ruback (1998) proposes a new approach: namely that of capital cash flows. It consists of finding the same result but by applying a simpler method that aims to make all of the cash available to investors (therefore including the tax advantages of interest charges). Arnold and North (2008) are more interested in making the DCF method more reliable. Based on the specific duration, they carry out a sensitivity study and calculate the effects of variations in the various parameters, which are initially subject to be critiqued as to their subjectivity. Finally, Shaffer (2006) adjusts the growth rate of the DCF method taking into account the risk of bankruptcy.

2.2.1. *Reconciliation of the traditional view with the Modigliani–Miller theorem*

Modigliani and Miller believe that the capital structure of a company does not have an impact on its value. Their model is essentially based on investor arbitration and their presupposed indifference to two opportunities that present the same risk and the same return. Including the effects of corporate taxes, they conclude that an increase in the level of debt increases the value of a business because of the tax deductibility of interest. Unlike their model, the traditional view is to determine an optimal level of debt (in terms of its effect on valuation). Dickinson and Kyuno (1977) propose a reconciliation between the traditional vision and that of Modigliani and Miller in the presence of taxation. Their objective is to demonstrate that an increase in the proportion of debt leads to a decrease in the average cost of capital (debt being a cheaper source of financing than equity) and, consequently, an increase in the value of company. Beyond a certain level of debt, the requirement for the company to make a profit implies an increased level of risk for holders of capital and for holders of debt. The latter therefore require a greater return on investment, which results in an increase in the average cost of capital. In addition, the taxation of individuals must be taken into account because they decide whether or not to invest, depending on the benefit they may derive from a potential leverage effect. In this context, Ferrar and Selwyn (1967) consider a tax rate based on the ownership interest in the company. Brennan (1970), on the other hand, takes into account trading opportunities in his study. Thus, the risk premium depends on the risk of the underlying security and the rate of dividends paid. The process of perfecting the optimization of the financial structure also applies to the DCF valuation method. Indeed, like Ruback (1998), it is possible to consider an alternative approach, that of capital cash flows (CCF), which seeks to preserve the very principle of discounting cash flows, while facilitating its implementation and by integrating the tax advantages which are linked to the deductibility of interest charges. In addition, Arnold and North (2008) prefer to focus on making the traditional DCF method more reliable by relying on the concept of duration. Through a sensitivity study, they determine the effects of variations in hypothetical parameters in order to measure the variation in cash flows.

2.2.1.1. *A general framework*

Dickinson and Kyuno (1977) assume that a company achieves result $\overline{X}$ continuously (without risk of default, without taxation, which involves an arbitration process and the distribution of profits). Let us note:

- V_U: market value of the deleveraged company U;
- V_L: market value of the indebted company L;
- S_L: market value of the company's equity L;
- B_L: market value of debt L;
- i: debt market interest rate;
- k_O: capitalization rate of capital income.

If an investor owns αV_U of capital of the firm U, their return (excluding tax considerations) is $\alpha\overline{X}$. Consider the total return of an investment that consists of αS_L parts equity and αB_L parts debt. Equity – after deduction of financial interest – has the value $\alpha(\overline{X} - iB_L)$ and debt αiB_L.

As the total return is also $\alpha(\overline{X} - iB_L) + \alpha iB_L = \alpha\overline{X}$, the hypothesis about arbitration implies that the investments in U and L have the same value, i.e.:

$$\alpha V_U = \alpha S_L + \alpha B_L = \alpha V_L \quad [2.1]$$

$$V_U = V_L \quad [2.2]$$

If the corporation tax is applied at rate t, the flow of net profit between corporation U and its investors is reduced to $\overline{X}(1-t)$. On the other hand, if R corresponds to interest payments on the debt, the corresponding flow for firm L is $(\overline{X} - R)(1-t) + R = \overline{X}(1-t) + tR$. The difference in value between the two companies is therefore obtained by capitalizing the tR tax "subsidy" by the appropriate rate, *i*:

$$V_L - V_U = \frac{tR}{i} = tB_L \quad [2.3]$$

$$V_L = V_U + tB_L \quad [2.4]$$

The equation can be compared with the traditional view, which includes a tax effect on non-corporate debt. This effect, y, remains positive up to a certain level, beyond which it decreases and becomes negative:

$$V_L = V_U + (y + t)B_L \quad [2.5]$$

Dickinson and Kyuno include in their model the tax on capital gains g, on dividends d_1 and on interest earned d_2. They also assume that investors are indifferent to a dividend payout or retained earnings and that the value of the company does not depend on the level of reinvestment. Thus, they consider two deleveraged companies, U_1 and U_2, to be identical in all points except in terms of dividend policy. U_1 preserves the tax saving $\overline{X}(1-t)$ within it, while U_2 again carries $b\overline{X}(1-t)$ and distributes $(1-b)\overline{X}(1-t)$ of dividends. In the presence of capital gains and income taxes, the net gains between the two companies and the investors are, respectively:

$$\overline{X}(1-t)(1-d_1) \text{ for } U_1 \quad [2.6]$$

$$\overline{X}(1-t)(1-d_1)(1-b) + b\overline{X}(1-t)(1-g) \text{ for } U_2 \quad [2.7]$$

By capitalizing these flows at the rate $k_1 = k_0(1-t)(1-d_1)$ corresponding to the tax rate after capitalization:

$$V_{U_1} = \frac{\bar{X}(1-t)(1-d_1)}{k_1} \qquad [2.8]$$

$$V_{U_2} = \frac{\bar{X}(1-t)(1-(1-b)d_1 + bg))}{k_1} \qquad [2.9]$$

$$\frac{V_{U_2}}{V_{U_1}} = \frac{1-((1-b)d_1 + bg)}{1-d_1} \qquad [2.10]$$

$$V_{U_2} = V_{U_1}\left[1 + \frac{b(d_1-g)}{1-d_1}\right] \qquad [2.11]$$

The difference in value between the two deleveraged companies increases (decreases) and the retention rate *b* increases (decreases) provided that $d_1 > g$ ($d_1 < g$).

Let us now consider two indebted companies L_1 and L_2, identical except in terms of dividend policy. The company L_1, with the equity capital S_L, distributes all the profits after tax in dividends, namely $(\bar{X} - R)(1-t)$.

The company L_2 again reports $b(\bar{X} - R)(1-t)$ and distributes $(1-b)$ $(\bar{X} - R)(1-t)$.

The net gains between the two companies and the investors are:

$$(\bar{X} - R)(1-t)(1-d_1)$$

and:

$$(\bar{X} - R)(1-t)(1-d_1)(1-b) + b(\bar{X} - R)(1-t)(1-g)$$

By capitalizing these two flows by the net return on equity e, and by income tax, we come to:

$$S_{L_1} = \frac{(\bar{X}-R)(1-t)(1-d_1)}{e} \qquad [2.12]$$

$$S_{L_2} = \frac{(\bar{X}-R)(1-t)(1-d_1)(1-b)+(\bar{X}-R)(1-t)(1-g)}{k_1} \qquad [2.13]$$

$$\frac{S_{L_2}}{S_{L_1}} = (1-b) + \frac{b(1-g)}{1-d_1} \quad [2.14]$$

$$S_{L_2} = S_{L_1}\left[1 + \frac{b\,(d_1-g)}{1-d_1}\right] \quad [2.15]$$

The value of L_2 increases (decreases) and the retention rate *b* increases (decreases) provided that $d_1 > g$ ($d_1 < g$). To introduce the effect of the dividend tax, d_2, we must consider a deleveraged company U and an indebted company L. The net gain flow is:

$$\bar{X}(1-t)(1-d_1) \text{ for U} \quad [2.16]$$

$$(\bar{X}-R)(1-t)(1-d_1) + r(1-d_2)$$

$$= \bar{X}(1-t)(1-d_1) + R[(1-d_2)-(1-t)(1-d_1)] \quad [2.17]$$

$$= \bar{X}(1-t)(1-d_1) + R[(1-d_1)t + (d_1-d_2)]$$

$$V_U = \frac{\bar{X}(1-t)(1-d_1)}{k_1} \quad [2.18]$$

$$V_L = \frac{\bar{X}(1-t)(1-d_1)}{k_1} + \left[\frac{(1-d_1)t + (d_1-d_2)}{(1-d_2)i}\right] R \quad [2.19]$$

In the second term of the second equation of [2.19], we capitalize by using $(1-d_2)i$, i.e. the interest rate of the debt after tax, since this "tax subsidy" is effectively a certain flow. By combining the results of equations [2.18] and [2.19], we find the following equation, which incorporates all of the effects in the presence of taxation:

$$V_L = V_U + \left[\frac{(1-d_1)t + (d_1-d_2)}{(1-d_2)i}\right] B_L + \frac{b(d_1-g)S_L}{1-d_1} \quad [2.20]$$

The increase in value from debt financing is only a function of *t* – as in the case of an individual investor – when $d_1 = d_2$. Indeed, the second term of equation [2.20] reduces tB_L. However, due to the last term of equation [2.20], the value increases (decreases) and the retention rate increases (decreases) if $d_1 > g$ ($d_1 < g$). It can also be noted that for the institutional investor, dividends are tax-deductible in order to avoid double taxation ($d_1 = 0$ and $d_2 = g = t$). Incorporating these values into equation [2.20] leads us to conclude that for such an investor, the tax advantage of "non-corporate" debt financing (which is negative) outweighs the tax advantage that comes from the company. Also, once the retention rate is increased (decreased), the value is decreased (increased). To summarize the results in a straightforward manner, we should assume that the retention rate *b* is constant for all companies with the same level of risk. The individual tax rate on the capital income, g′, is therefore the weighted average:

$$g' = (1 - b)d_1 + bg \quad [2.21]$$

$$V_U = \frac{\bar{X}(1-t)(1-g')}{k_2} \quad [2.22]$$

where:

$$k_2 = k_0(1 - t)(1 - g') \quad [2.23]$$

$$V_L = \frac{\bar{X}(1-t)(1-g')}{k_2} + \left[\frac{(1-d_2)-(1-t)(1-g')}{(1-d_2)i}\right] R \quad [2.24]$$

$$V_L = V_U + tBL - \frac{(1-t)(d_2 g')B_L}{(1-d_2)} \quad [2.25]$$

$$V_L - tB_L = V_U - \frac{(1-t)(d_2 - g')B_L}{(1-d_2)} \quad [2.26]$$

$$y = -\frac{(1-t)(d_2-g')B_L}{(1-d_2)} \quad [2.27]$$

The second term on the right-hand side of equation [2.26] is a measure of the “non-corporate” tax effect of debt financing. When $d_2 > g'$, this term is negative and the corporate tax saving of debt financing is compensation. The taxation of individuals is therefore supposed to impact the financial policy of companies.

2.2.1.2. *The impact of personal taxation on optimal financial policy*

Dickinson and Kyonu (1977) believe that investors arbitrate their decision to participate according to the possible benefit of personal leverage. When considering the effects of the taxation of individuals on the financial policy of a company, Farrar and Selwyn (1967) focus, however, only on the net income received by an investor at a tax rate that depends on the share held in the company. Their use of this concept of net income as a criterion for best value overlooks the trading opportunities that are open in markets to an investor who does not adhere to a particular financial policy. Thus,

Brennan (1970) extends the analysis of Modigliani and Miller by including personal taxation as a whole and observes impact on a company's financial policy. Trading opportunities are taken into account, by applying the principle of market valuation, while the impact of alternative financial policies on the value of the company can be calculated.

2.2.1.2.1. Investor personal leverage and maximization of investor income after tax

According to Dickinson and Kyonu (1977), an investor who holds αS_L of the capital of a firm L will receive a return of $\alpha(X - R)(1 - t)(1 - g')$. By investing αV_U in the capital of a firm U, a return of $\alpha X(1 - t)(1 - g')$ is obtained. If the last investment is financed through a loan $\alpha(1 - t)(1 - g')B_L$, which involves an interest of $\alpha R(1 - t)(1 - g')$, its total return will be $\alpha(X - R)(1 - t)(1 - g')$. This is exactly the return on the first investment, and we can therefore conclude that the amounts invested in both situations are identical:

$$\begin{aligned} \alpha S_L &= \alpha V_U - (1 - t)(1 - g')B_L \\ &= \alpha V_U - \alpha(1 - t)B_L + \alpha(1 - t)g'B_L \\ &= \alpha V_U - \alpha B_L + \alpha B_L + \alpha(1 - t)g'B_L \end{aligned} \quad [2.28]$$

And so:

$$V_L = V_U + tB_L + (1 - t)g'B_L \quad [2.29]$$

$$V_L - tB_L = V_U + (1 - t)g'B_L \quad [2.30]$$

$$y = (1 - t)g' \quad [2.31]$$

Equation [2.27] should be compared to equation [2.31]. Both expressions give the effect of the personal tax, y, of debt financing with and without investor leverage. If the market is dominated by aggressive investors with significant risk aversion, equation [2.31] will be applied. Besides corporate tax, the advantage is to increase the level of debt. Conversely, if the market is dominated by more conservative investors, equation [2.27] will be favored and an increase in debt will wipe out the corporate tax advantage. In practice, it is impossible to define the direction and the magnitude of the personal tax effect, since it depends on investor preferences and the degree of taxation. Dickinson and Kyonu consider that the best effect should satisfy the following inequality:

$$-\frac{(1-t)(d_2-g\prime)}{1-d_2} < y < (1-t)g' \quad [2.32]$$

Farrar and Selwyn (1967) assess corporate financial policies with respect to income after-tax that is received by an investor with a stake in a firm. And so it follows:

– Y: net income flow (including capital gains) available to an investor who holds a share, net of any interest and taxes (personal or corporate);

– X: operating profit per share of the company before payment of interest and taxes;

– r: market interest rate;

– D_c: amount of corporate debt per share;

– D_p: amount of personal debt per share;

– T_e, T_p, T_g: Marginal tax rate on corporations, income and capital gains.

A first strategy consists of paying the profits in the form of dividends and taxing them through income tax. Thus, the net income per share of the investor is:

$$Y = \left[(X - rD_c)(1 - T_c) - rD_p\right](1 - T_p) \quad [2.33]$$

The costs after-tax to the investor of corporate and personal debt are:

$$\frac{\partial Y}{\partial D_p} = r(1 - T_p) \quad [2.34]$$

$$\frac{\partial Y}{\partial D_c} = r(1 - T_p)(1 - T_c) \quad [2.35]$$

The investor's net income per share is reduced less by additional corporate debt than by additional personal debt, because of the additional corporate interest tax shield, which is offered by corporate tax. Thus, corporate debt is cheaper than personal debt for all investors, regardless of the marginal interest rate applied.

A second strategy is to convert the profit into capital gain and tax it at the investor's level, at the capital gains tax rate. In this case, the net income available to the investor will be:

$$Y = (X - rD_c)(1 - T_c)(1 - T_g) - rD_p(1 - T_p) \quad [2.36]$$

The costs of personal and corporate debt are:

$$\frac{\partial Y}{\partial D_p} = r(1 - T_p) \quad [2.37]$$

$$\frac{\partial Y}{\partial D_c} = r(1 - T_p)(1 - T_g) \quad [2.38]$$

From there, corporate debt is cheaper for the investor only if:

$$(1 - T_c)(1 - T_g) < (1 - T_p) \text{ or } T_p < T_c + T_g + T_c T_g \quad [2.39]$$

Equation [2.39] indicates that the relative effects of corporate and personal debt on the net earnings per share received by the investor depend on their marginal tax rates T_p and T_g. In general, investors with a low-tax bracket will find the impact of corporate debt on their net income relatively less favorable than those with a high-tax bracket. Thus, if the criterion for maximizing the net profit per share received by investors is accepted, we can conclude that it will always be optimal for a company to use residual profits to buy back shares rather than pay dividends, as long as the marginal tax rate on investors' dividends exceeds that on capital gains. In addition, corporate debt will benefit investors in a company that pays dividends, although the value of the debt may directly depend on the marginal tax rate T_p of some investors. For a company that does not pay dividends, different financial policies may be optimal for different groups of investors, depending on their marginal tax rates. For example, investors with a marginal tax rate for whom $T_p > T_c + T_g + T_c T_g$ will probably prefer the company to implement a "zero-debt" strategy, in order to maximize the amount of debt that investors can contract themselves, consistent with their desire for total debt per share. On the other hand, investors with a low marginal tax rate will seem to prefer the company to implement a "maximum debt" strategy. If such a strategy results in excessive leverage per share from an investor's perspective, it can still be partially offset by their personal loans. However, in addition to coming across diverse opinions as to the optimality of the financial policy to be implemented (according to the group of investors to which one belongs), the criterion for maximizing the income after-tax paid to them implies that they have no choice: they remain shareholders and are therefore only interested in income per share. By adopting a more realistic assumption – i.e. thinking that investors have the ability to not only borrow and lend but also sell (or buy) their securities in the market – and assuming that opportunities are ultimately independent of decisions of a single firm, the welfare of investors can be maximized by optimizing the market value of the firm. Thus, the potential investor conflicts raised by Farrar and Selwyn are no longer relevant as long as the opportunities to "trade" in the market on the part of investors have been accepted. In other words, investors can perform their arbitration. As a result of this, the approach proposed by Farrar and Selwyn reveals itself to be too static, because it does not take into account the impact of issuing corporate debt on the net income Y of the investor, while neglecting the principle of company valuation.

2.2.1.2.2. Market valuation in a situation of uncertainty

Analysis from Brennan (1970) builds on the generalized CAPM from Sharpe (1964), Lintner (1965) and Mossin (1966) by incorporating the effects of tax on income through dividends and on capital gains. We then assume that the utility functions $U_i(i = 1,\ldots,m)$ of investors depend on the mean V_i and the variance $S^2{}_i$ of the returns after-tax from the portfolios:

$$\left.\begin{aligned} U_i &= U_i(V_i, S^2{}_i) \\ U'_i &= \frac{\partial U_i}{\partial V_i} > 0 \\ U''_i &= \frac{\partial U_i}{\partial S^2{}_i} < 0 \end{aligned}\right\} \text{ for } i = 1,\ldots, m \qquad [2.40]$$

Investors are supposed to trade n + 1 securities:

– security 0 is supposed to have an initial value and a known terminal value q;

– n remaining securities have an initial value p_j ($j = 1,\ldots, n$); an unknown terminal value π_j;

– each security j ($j = 1,\ldots, n$) gives the right to a final dividend d_j already known at the start of the period;

– the terminal values of the securities have a covariance S_{jk} (j = 1,..., n);

– each investor *i* (i = 1,..., m) has an initial allocation of X^0_{ji} securities *j* (j = 1,..., n), and, by trading with other investors, we arrive at a situation of equilibrium in the position of the assets at X_{ji}(j = 1,..., n);

– each investor has a marginal tax rate on t_{di} dividends and on t_{gi} capital gains that are constant and independent of the choice of portfolio.

The expected return after-tax on the portfolio of investor *i* is:

$$V_i = \sum_{j=1}^{n}\left[\pi_j - (\pi_j - p_j)t_{gi} + d_j(1 - t_{di})\right]X_{ji} + [q - (q-1)t_{di}]X_{oi} \qquad [2.41]$$

And the various of return after-tax is:

$$S^2{}_i = \sum_{j=1}^{n}\sum_{k=1}^{n} S_{jk}\, X_{ji}X_{ki}(1 - t_{gi})^2 \qquad [2.42]$$

And so, the investor maximizes their utility function:

$$U_i = U_i(V_i, S^2{}_i) \qquad [2.43]$$

This utility function is subject to the investor's budget constraint:

$$\sum_{j=1}^{n} p_j\left(X_{ji} - X^0{}_{ji}\right) + (X_{0i} - X^0{}_{0i}) = 0 \qquad [2.44]$$

The first-order conditions of maximum constraints are obtained by using the Langrangian expression:

$$L = U_i(V_i, S^2{}_i) - \lambda\left[\sum_{j=1}^{n} p_j\left(X_{ji} - X^0{}_{ji}\right) + (X_{0i} - X^0{}_{0i})\right] \qquad [2.45]$$

Any by setting its partial derivative to be equal to zero for $X_{ji}(j = 1, \ldots, n)$ and λ gives:

$$\frac{\partial L}{\partial X_{ji}} = U'_i\frac{\partial V_i}{\partial X_{ji}} + U''_i\frac{\partial S^2{}_i}{\partial X_{ji}} - \lambda p_j = 0 \qquad [2.46]$$

$$\frac{\partial L}{\partial \lambda} = \sum_{j=1}^{n} p_j\left(X_{ji} - X^0{}_{ji}\right) + (X_{0i} - X^0{}_{0i}) = 0 \qquad [2.47]$$

When looking at [2.41], we note that:

$$\frac{\partial V_i}{\partial X_{oi}} = q - (q-1)t_{di} \qquad [2.48]$$

$$\frac{\partial V_i}{\partial X_{ji}} = \pi_j - (\pi_j - p_j)t_{gi} + d_j(1 - t_{di}) \qquad [2.49]$$

And when looking at [2.42], we note that:

$$\frac{\partial S^2{}_i}{\partial X_{oi}} = 0 \qquad [2.50]$$

$$\frac{\partial S^2{}_i}{\partial X_{ji}} = 2\sum_{k=1}^{n} S_{jk}\, X_{ji} X_{ki} (1 - t_{gi})^2 \qquad [2.51]$$

And so, we obtain these maximum constraints as conditions in addition to that of the budget (equation [2.47]):

$$\frac{\partial L}{\partial X_{oi}} = U'_i[q - (q-1)t_{di}] - \lambda = 0 \qquad [2.52]$$

$$\begin{aligned}\frac{\partial L}{\partial X_{ji}} &= U'_i \pi_j - (\pi_j - p_j)t_{gi} + d_j(1 - t_{di}) \\ &+ U''_i\left[2\sum_{k=1}^{n} S_{jk}\,(1 - t_{gi})^2 - X_{ki}\right] - \lambda p_j = 0\end{aligned} \qquad [2.53]$$

By eliminating λ between [2.52] and [2.53] and through a process of simplification, we get:

$$\sum_{k=1}^{n} S_{jk}\, X_{ki} = \frac{w_i}{(1 - t_{gi})^2}\begin{bmatrix}\pi_j(1 - t_{gi}) + p_j t_{gi} + d_j(1 - t_{di}) \\ - p_j(q - (q-1)t_{di})\end{bmatrix} \qquad [2.54]$$

where $w_i = -\frac{1}{2}\frac{U'_i}{U''_i}$ is proportional to the investor's marginal rate of substitution between the expected return and the variance. Assuming that the second-order conditions for the maximum constraints are satisfied, equation [2.54] gives the equilibrium relation between the covariance of the return of the security *j* (j = 1,…, n) and the risk premium after expected tax by security *j*. The *n* equations of [2.54], which are correlated with the budget constraint equation [2.47], are sufficient to determine the equilibrium of the investor's portfolio in the holding of their n + 1 securities. We may note that when w_i enters as a constant in [2.54], the investor's relative holdings *n* securities are independent of the exact model of their utility function but not of their marginal tax rate t_{di} and t_{gi}. Market equilibrium is based first of all on the fact that each investor has a portfolio equilibrium, i.e. that equations [2.47] and [2.54] are verified for each of them (i = 1,…, m) and second that the securities market allows:

$$\sum_{i=1}^{m} X_{ji} = \sum_{i=1}^{m} X^{0}{}_{ji} = X^{0}{}_{j} \qquad [2.55]$$

where $X^0{}_j$ is the exceptional offer of security *j*. Then, by adding [2.54] on all the investors:

$$h \sum_{k=1}^{n} S_{jk} X^{0}{}_{k} = \left[\pi_j + d_j - qp_j\right] - T_g\left[\pi_j - p_j\right] - T_d\left[d_j - p_j(q-1)\right] \qquad [2.56]$$

where:

$$h = \left[\sum_{i=1}^{m} \frac{w_i}{(1-t_{gi})^2}\right]^{-1} \qquad [2.57]$$

$$T_g = \left[\sum_{i=1}^{m} \frac{w_i t_{gi}}{(1-t_{gi})^2}\right]\left[\sum_{i=1}^{m} \frac{w_i}{(1-t_{gi})^2}\right]^{-1} \qquad [2.58]$$

$$T_d = \left[\sum_{i=1}^{m} \frac{w_i t_{di}}{(1-t_{gi})^2}\right]\left[\sum_{i=1}^{m} \frac{w_i}{(1-t_{gi})^2}\right]^{-1} \qquad [2.59]$$

We note that T_d and T_g are weighted averages of the tax rate on dividends and on investor capital gains, where the weights depend on the marginal rate of substitution of investors between the expected return and the variance of that return. Let us define new variables:

– $r = q - 1$ the risk-free interest rate;

– $\delta_j = \frac{d_j}{p_j}$ the eventual return of the dividend on security *j* (j = 1,…, n);

– $R = \frac{\pi_j + d_j + p_j}{p_j}$ the return on investment on security *j* (j = 1,…, n).

We note that:

$$\sum_{k=1}^{n} \frac{S_{jk}}{p_j} X^{0}{}_{k} = M \sum_{k=1}^{n} Q_k COV(R_j R_k) \qquad [2.60]$$

where M is the total market value of securities and Q_k (k = 1,…, n) and part of the security *k* in the total market value. Then, by dividing [2.56] by p_j, and by transposing the terms and making the substitutions of returns:

$$R_j - r = hM\sum_{k=1}^{n} Q_k COV(R_j R_k) + T_d(\delta_j - r) + T_g(R_j - r) \quad [2.61]$$

$$= hM\sum_{k=1}^{n} Q_k COV(R_j R_k) + T(\delta_j - r) \quad [2.62]$$

where $H = \frac{h}{(1-T_g)}$ et $T = \frac{T_d - T_g}{1-T_g}$.

Finally, equation [2.62] can be simplified by noting that $\sum_{k=1}^{n} Q_k M R_k = R_m$, where R_m is the rate of return on the entire market portfolio:

$$M\sum_{k=1}^{n} Q_k . COV(R_j R_k) = COV(R_j R_m) \quad [2.63]$$

and [2.62] becomes:

$$R_j - r = H.COV(R_j R_m) + T(\delta_j - r) \quad [2.64]$$

Equation [2.64] therefore expresses the basic principle of market valuation in a situation of uncertainty when investors have different tax rates, and it shows that the risk premium that is required or expected on security *j* (j = 1, …, n) (R_j - r) is a function of the risk characteristics of the security $COV(R_j, R_m)$ and its expected dividend rate δ_j. Intuitively, this result indicates that for a given level of risk, investors demand a higher total return on a security; the dividend rate must be higher since its tax rate is higher than that of capital gains.

2.2.1.3. *Reconsidering the Modigliani–Miller theorem*

2.2.1.3.1. The dividend payment constraint

Let us consider that there is no growth and that the future can be looked at as a series of identical periods where, in each of them, the market equilibrium condition of equation [2.64] is expected. In addition, at each period, the company receives a flow of operating income X, which is taxed at the IS rate τ. The company is supposed to pay a dividend D and buy back or issue shares at the end of each period while its market value V is constant. Assuming that investors' risk taking and tax rates remain constant over time, expected future gains will be capitalized at a constant rate ρ. The possibility of a change in the value of the business due to a recapitalization of expected future earnings is excluded. Therefore, the end-of-period value of the company V_t, after dividends have been paid but before the shares have been redeemed or issued, will be equal to the value of the company at the start of the period, plus the result of operating net of tax minus dividends, namely:

$$V_t = V + X(1-\tau) - D \qquad [2.65]$$

Let us make R the rate of return of securities of the company:

$$1 + R = \frac{V_t + D}{V} \qquad [2.66]$$

and:

$$COV(R, R_m) = COV\left[\frac{V + X(1-\tau), R_m}{V, R_m}\right] = COV\left[\frac{X(1-\tau)}{V, R_m}\right] \qquad [2.67]$$

As a result, the value of company V can be written as the capitalized value of expected gains after tax:

$$V = \frac{X(1-\tau)}{\rho} \qquad [2.68]$$

where the rate of capitalization ρ is given by the condition of an equal [2.64]:

$$\begin{aligned} \rho &= r + H.COV(R, R_m) + T\left[\frac{D}{V} - r\right] \\ &= r + H.COV\left[\frac{X(1-\rho)}{V, R_m}\right] + T\left[\frac{D}{V} - r\right] \end{aligned} \qquad [2.69]$$

where $\frac{D}{V}$ will be the prospect of the dividend yield on the company's securities. Then, by substituting ρ in [2.69] and adjusting it, we reach:

$$V = \frac{X(1-\tau) - H.COV[X(1-\tau), R_m] - TD}{r(1-T)} \qquad [2.70]$$

Equation [2.70] is a general valuation equation for the company that expresses its value as a function of the flow of net income from operations, and the amount of dividends paid in each period. To calculate the effect of alternative dividend policies on the value of the firm, we must partially differentiate [2.70] from D:

$$\frac{\partial V}{\partial D} = \frac{-T}{r(1-T)} \qquad [2.71]$$

Equation [2.71] demonstrates that if the market value maximization criterion is accepted and if T> 0, investors have no interest in receiving dividends: share repurchases are preferred regardless of marginal tax rates. However, since most companies in fact pay regular dividends, such behavior needs to be streamlined, so that it is a real or a perceived constraint. Thus, it is necessary to presume that the company is subject to such a constraint.

Let us suppose that a company possesses an amount of bonds B whose interest rate is r. The market value of its capital is:

$$E = V - B \qquad [2.72]$$

But E can also be considered as the net income expected by capital owners $(X - rB)(1 - \tau)$, capitalized at a rate of ρ_E depending on the risk and the composition of the capital income flow:

$$E = \frac{(X-rB)(1-\tau)}{\rho_E} \qquad [2.73]$$

$$\rho_E = r + H\ COV\left[\frac{X(1-\tau)}{E,R_m}\right] + T\left[\frac{D}{E} - r\right] \qquad [2.74]$$

$$E = \frac{(X-rB)(1-\tau)-HCOV[X(\&-\tau),R_m]-TD}{r(1-T)} \qquad [2.75]$$

The constraint on the systematic share buyback can be written as such:

$$D + (1-\tau)rB \geq X(1-\tau) \qquad [2.76]$$

Equation [2.76] implies that the amount paid in dividends and the net interest payment are at least as large as the average flow of net income. We will note that:

$$V = B + E \qquad [2.77]$$

$$\frac{dV}{dB} = 1 + \frac{dE}{dB} \qquad [2.78]$$

Let us consider the effects of alternative debt levels on enterprise value under two constraints.

1) The constraint on the share buyback is not linked so that:

$$D + (1 + \tau)rB > X(1 + \tau) \quad [2.79]$$

So, based on expression [2.75], we can deduce that:

$$\frac{dE}{dB} = -\frac{1-\tau}{1-T} \quad [2.80]$$

And by looking at expression [2.80], we can deduce that:

$$\frac{dV}{dB} = \frac{\tau-T}{1-T} \quad [2.81]$$

Equation [2.81] shows that a strong leverage strategy will maximize enterprise value and therefore be beneficial to all investors as long as the corporate tax rate τ exceeds the effective market tax rate T. However, the relative advantage of corporate debt is reduced by the existence of investor tax ($T > 0$).

2) The constraint on the repurchase of shares is linked so that:

$$D + (1 + \tau)rB = X(1 + \tau) \quad [2.82]$$

$$\frac{dD}{dB} = -(1 - \tau)r \quad [2.83]$$

So, the issuance of debt reduces the amount of dividends that must be paid by the interest cost of the net debt. Taking this into account:

$$\begin{aligned} \frac{dV}{dB} &= \frac{\partial V}{\partial B} + \frac{\partial V}{\partial D}\frac{dD}{dB} \\ &= \frac{\tau-T}{1-T} + \frac{T(1-\tau)}{1-T} \quad [2.84] \\ &= r \end{aligned}$$

And this is precisely the result obtained by Modigliani and Miller by neglecting the taxation of investors: if an amount of B bonds are issued, the value of the company is increased by τB. Thus, if the company is subject to a constraint on share buyback, Modigliani–Miller's cost of capital proposals are unaffected by the existence of investor tax. This is based on the relationship between the amount of debt issued and the amount of dividends paid over the same period. The share buyback excludes the issuance of bonds, but there is a link between the debt issued and the dividends paid over the period that affects the valuation.

2.2.1.3.2. The effect of a debt issuance on enterprise value

Let V be the current value of the company and ΔB be the expected issuance of debt at the end of the first period. It is assumed that the company pays a constant dividend, does not incur other debt in subsequent periods and does not buy back shares. Thus, V_t is the enterprise value at the end of a period after debt has been issued and dividends paid.

We thus reach:

$$\frac{dV_t}{d\Delta B} = r \qquad [2.85]$$

$$\frac{dV'_t}{d\Delta B} = r \qquad [2.86]$$

The total investor return throughout this period is:

$$\frac{V'_t + X_1(1-\tau) - V}{V} \qquad [2.87]$$

The market balance makes it necessary for the expected value of equation [2.87] to be equal to:

$$r(1-T) + H.\,COV\left[\frac{V'_t + X_1(1-\tau), R_m}{V, R_m}\right] - T\frac{D_1}{V} \qquad [2.88]$$

where D_1 is the amount of dividends paid in the first period. Then, by equaling [2.87] and [2.88] and by resolving V, we get:

$$V = \frac{V'_t + X_1(1-\tau)}{1+r(1-T)} - \frac{H\,COV[V'_t + X_1(1-\tau), R_m] - TD_1}{1+r(1-T)} \qquad [2.89]$$

The constraint on the share buyback for the first period can be written as:

$$D_1 + (1-\tau)rB \geq X_1(1-\tau) + \Delta B \qquad [2.90]$$

Note that equation [2.90] explicitly excludes the use of the issue of bonds with a view to repurchasing shares.

$$\frac{dV}{d\Delta B} = \frac{\partial V}{\partial \Delta B} + \frac{\partial V}{\partial D_1}\frac{dD_1}{d\Delta B} \qquad [2.91]$$

Equation [2.91] shows that the total impact of expected debt issuance on enterprise value has two components: a direct impact $\frac{\partial V}{\partial \Delta B}$ and an indirect impact $\frac{\partial V}{\partial D_1}\frac{dD_1}{d\Delta B}$ due to the consequent modifications of the dividends of the first period. If the redemption constraint of equation [2.90] is prohibited, $\frac{dD_1}{d\Delta B} = 1$ and:

$$\frac{dV}{d\Delta B} = \frac{\tau - T}{1 + r(1 - T)} \qquad [2.92]$$

Thus, when the repurchase constraint is prohibited, equation [2.92] shows that the issuance of debt will be advantageous if the IS rate τ is greater than T. However, when the repurchase of shares requires the issuance of bonds in order to pay dividends, the initial advantage of incorporating debt into the capital structure is diminished, because even though the enterprise value tends to increase by saving taxes (thanks to the bond issuance), the higher taxation of investors reduces this effect, to the extent that they have to pay the increase in dividends for the first period (brought about by the issuance of bonds).

After trying to refine Modigliani and Miller's approach with regard to the financial structure and its impact on enterprise value, taking into account, in particular, the taxation of individuals, we may question if it is actually possible to optimize valuation methods by discounting cash flows (especially DCFs). In this way, the objective is to propose an alternative method or, at least, to make the assumed parameters of the DCF model more reliable. The DCF model is majorly criticized for its subjectivity, which, beyond that, can generate significant variations in calculations from one analyst to another in the quest for fair corporate value.

2.2.2. *Optimizing the valuation methods*

Ruback (1998) presents an alternative to the traditional DCF method for assessing risky cash flows and obtaining enterprise value. The capital cash flow method ultimately provides an enterprise value that is identical to that reached in the free cash flow method. It exists because of the simplicity of its implementation. It therefore lends itself more easily to the valuation of companies that have been subject to transactions with a high leverage effect, companies that have undergone restructuring or major financing projects or, finally, any other operation in which the capital structure has been largely affected, because the CCF method consists of including all the cash available to fund providers, therefore including the tax advantages linked to interest charges. These reduce taxable income. As a result, corporation tax decreases, resulting in an increase in cash flow after-tax. In other words, the capital cash flows are equivalent to the free cash flows to which we add the tax deductibility of interest charges. Because it is included in cash flows, the appropriate discount rate must then be a pre-tax rate to avoid double counting. It corresponds to the WACC before tax. Thus, unlike the DCF method, the various parameters of the capital cash flow method are not subject to adjustments, depending on the situation. Indeed, unlike an essential re-estimate of the WACC in the event of variations in the financial structure over time, the impact of these modifications in the CCF method is zero, insofar as the tax advantages of interest charges are included in the cash flows considered and that the risk-free rate of the assets is a fixed discount rate. Without proposing an alternative valuation method to that of DCF, Arnold and North (2008) seek to make this approach more reliable by carrying out a sensitivity study, based on the concept of duration, in order to calculate the effects of variations in the assumed parameters and to propose a measure of the variation in cash flows. Shaffer (2006), for his part, integrates the risk of bankruptcy through an adjusted growth rate.

2.2.2.1. *Tax deductibility of interest charges and residual profits*

In the DCF method, the tax deductibility of interest decreases the WACC, which, by definition, is after tax. Tax benefits related to interest charges are therefore excluded from free cash flows. Problems arise when the WACC is impacted by large variations in the capital structure. If the latter is simple, i.e. composed of classic bank debt and ordinary shares, the capital cash flows are equal to the flows available to shareholders, in addition to the interest paid to debt holders. Ruback (1998) thus takes up the idea, which was developed in his previous work (Ruback 1986), which dictates that the tax advantages of interest charges associated with risk-free cash flows are equivalent to the increase in cash flows generated by these same benefits, or a decrease in the discount rate, i.e. the risk-free rate after tax. The analysis thus presents similar results for risky cash flows: they can be obtained by using the CCF or DCF method, for which the tax benefits are added to the FCF in the discount rate. Although free and capital cash flows treat the tax deductibility of interest charges differently, the two methods are algebraically comparable.

To illustrate, let us determine the WACC before tax:

$$\mathrm{WACC}_{\text{before tax}} = \mathrm{k}\,\frac{\mathrm{E}}{\mathrm{EV}} + \mathrm{i}\,\frac{\mathrm{D}}{\mathrm{EV}} \quad [2.93]$$

where:

– $\mathrm{k} = \mathrm{r_f} + \beta_{\mathrm{E}}\mathrm{R_P}$;

– $i = \mathrm{r_f} + \beta_{\mathrm{D}}\mathrm{R_P}$;

– $\mathrm{r_f}$ = risk-free rate;

– $\mathrm{R_P}$ = risk premium;

– β_{E} et β_{D}= equity and debt betas.

And so:

$$\mathrm{WACC}_{\text{before tax}} = (r_f + \beta_E R_P)\,\frac{\mathrm{E}}{\mathrm{EV}} + (r_f + \beta_D R_P)\,\frac{\mathrm{D}}{\mathrm{EV}} \quad [2.94]$$

$$\mathrm{WACC}_{\text{before tax}} = r_f\left(\frac{E}{EV} + \frac{D}{EV}\right) + R_P\left(\beta_E\,\frac{E}{EV} + \beta_D\,\frac{D}{EV}\right) \quad [2.95]$$

and:

$$\frac{\mathrm{E}}{\mathrm{EV}} + \frac{\mathrm{D}}{\mathrm{EV}} = 1 \quad [2.96]$$

Moreover, note the beta of the deleveraged asset:

$$\beta_{\mathrm{U}} = \beta_{\mathrm{E}}\,\frac{\mathrm{E}}{\mathrm{EV}} + \beta_{\mathrm{D}}\,\frac{\mathrm{D}}{\mathrm{EV}} \quad [2.97]$$

And so:

$$\mathrm{WACC}_{\text{before tax}} = \mathrm{K_A} = \mathrm{r_f} + \mathrm{R_P}\beta_{\mathrm{U}} \quad [2.98]$$

Note that the discount rate does not depend on the financial structure and should not be recalculated according to its variations. This therefore means that, in the CCF method, debt-to-enterprise value and equity-to-enterprise value ratios do not need to be estimated. Therefore, this eliminates much of the complexity that we encounter when evaluating from the DCF method. Let us remember:

$$V_{FCF} = \frac{FCF}{K} \qquad [2.99]$$

where:

$$K = WACC = k\frac{E}{EV} + i(1-\tau)\frac{D}{EV}$$

Capital cash flow is the cash flow expected by all fundraisers that incorporate the forecasts of the financing policy, including the tax deductibility of interest charges. Since free cash flows measure the cash flows available to shareholders, it suffices to add the tax deductibility mentioned above to them to obtain capital cash flows:

$$CCF = FCF + \tau iD \qquad [2.100]$$

where τiD corresponds to the tax deductibility of interest, with τ being the corporate tax rate, *i* the interest rate and D the amount of debt. The present value of capital cash flows is obtained by discounting them at the expected rate of return on the assets. Thus:

$$V_{CCF} = \frac{FCF+\tau iD}{r_f+R_P\beta_U} \qquad [2.101]$$

$$V_{CCF} = \frac{FCF+\tau iD}{K_A} \qquad [2.102]$$

We can therefore show that algebraically the two methods are equivalent:

$$V_{FCF} = \frac{FCF}{k\frac{E}{EV}+i(1-\tau)\frac{D}{EV}} \qquad [2.103]$$

$$V_{FCF}\left(K_A - \tau i\frac{D}{EV}\right) = FCF \qquad [2.104]$$

$$V_{FCF} = \frac{FCF+\tau iD}{K_A} \qquad [2.105]$$

Therefore, the choice to use one of the two methods depends on the degree of ease and therefore on the probability of error when determining the parameters. Thus, the way in which the cash flow projection is carried out usually dictates the method. Ruback recommends the free cash flow method during a simple valuation, where the cash flows do not include tax deductibility of interest charges and when the financing strategy is stable over time. On the other hand, when the cash flows incorporate detailed information about the financing plan or in complex tax situations, the CCF method would seem to be more effective.

The adjusted present value method developed by Myers (1974), or the APV method[1], is generally calculated by proceeding to the sum of the free cash flows discounted at the cost of the assets and the tax deductibility of the interest charges discounted at the cost of debt[2]. The APV method distinguishes the net present value that the project generates if it is fully financed by equity, and the present value of cash flows related to other sources of finance, for which the present value of tax savings due to the use of debt is the most important part. The discount rate is the cost of capital. Ruback measures the differences in value that reside between an APV and CCF valuation, assuming infinite cash flows and tax deductibility of interest charges as a proportion, γ, of the value of equity E.

$$\frac{V_{APV}}{V_{CCF}} = \frac{1+\gamma\left(\frac{K_A}{i}\right)}{1+\gamma} \qquad [2.106]$$

Thus, Ruback presents the results of his study and notes that the value obtained by the APV method is higher than that obtained from the CCF method because it confers a greater value on the tax deductibility of interest charges.

		K_A/i		
		1.25	**1.5**	**1.75**
γ	**10%**	2%	5%	7%
	15%	3%	7%	10%
	20%	4%	8%	13%

Table 2.1. *Percentage difference between the values obtained by the VPA and those obtained by the CCF (VAPV/vCCF)*

1 APV: adjusted present value.

2 Note that Myers expresses the term compressed APV to precisely describe Ruback's CCF method as the tax deductibility of interest charges is, in this case, discounted to the cost of the assets.

For example, if K_A is at 15% and i is at 10%, their ratio is 1:5. By assuming an IS rate of 36% and a gearing of 42%, the value of tax deductibility for interest charges is about 15%. We are then in the middle of Table 2.1 and we observe that the APV method provides a 7% higher valuation than the CCF method does.

When debt is assumed to be constant, the beta of the tax deductibility of interest charges is the beta of the debt. Furthermore, this implies that the appropriate discount rate for the tax deductibility of interest charges is the interest rate on the debt, the rate used in the APV method. It also implies that the tax benefits provided by interest charges are assumed to be less risky than assets, because the level of debt is assumed to be fixed. Indeed:

$$V_{DFI,t} = \tau V_{D,t} \quad [2.107]$$

where:

– V_{DFI} is the value of tax deductibility of interests;

– τ is the IS rate;

– $V_{D,t}$ is the amount of debt for period t;

– and:

$$\beta_{DFI} = \frac{Cov(V_{DFI,t}, R_M)}{V_{DFI,t-1} Var(R_M)} \quad [2.108]$$

$$\beta_{DFI} = \frac{Cov(V_{D,t}, R_M)}{V_{D,t-1} Var(R_M)} \quad [2.109]$$

$$\beta_{DFI} = \beta_D \quad [2.110]$$

When debt is assumed to be proportional to enterprise value, the beta of the tax deductibility of interest charges is the beta of assets (which are deleveraged). This implies that the appropriate discount rate is the cost of assets, the rate used in the CCF method. It also results in taxes having no effect on equity beta in asset beta (they cancel out on both sides of the fraction).

$$V_{DFI,t} = \tau V_{D,t} = \tau \delta V_U \quad [2.111]$$

where:

– δ represents the coefficient;

– V_U is the value of the indebted company;

– and:

$$\beta_{DFI} = \frac{Cov(V_{DFI,t}, R_M)}{V_{DFI,t-1} Var(R_M)} \quad [2.112]$$

$$\beta_{DFI} = \frac{Cov(\tau\delta V_{U,t}, R_M)}{\tau\delta V_{U,t-1} Var(R_M)} \quad [2.113]$$

$$\beta_{DFI} = \beta_U \quad [2.114]$$

In the event that the amount of debt is not fixed, the risk of tax benefits depends on the risk of payment and systematic changes in the amount of debt. Since the risk of an indebted enterprise is a weighted average of the risk of a deleveraged enterprise and the risk of the tax benefits of interest charges, the presence of a lower risk that relates to the tax benefits of interest charges reduces the risk of the indebted company. In this way, a tax adjustment must be made for a deleveraged company on the beta of the stock to calculate the beta of the assets. The CCF method, akin to the DCF method, assumes that debt is proportional to enterprise value. The greater the latter, the more the debt will occupy an important part in the financial structure. And the larger the debt, the greater the tax benefits associated with interest payments. Thus, the risk of the tax benefits of interest charges depends on the risk of the debt as well as its variations. When debt is a fixed proportion of enterprise value, the tax benefits have the same risk as the enterprise, with debt not affecting its beta. Therefore, no tax adjustment needs to be made to calculate the beta of the asset.

Therefore, the difference between the CCF and APV method depends on the debt assumptions made. The CCF method and, beyond that, the DCF method assume a debt proportional to value. The APV method assumes a fixed debt, independent of value. Ruback argues that debt cannot literally be proportional to value, for example, when dealing with companies that are in difficult times where the risk of debt increases, thus interfering with proportionality. However, Graham and Harvey (1999) observed in their study that 80% of large companies have a target debt-to-enterprise value ratio. We can therefore assume that the CCF or DCF method can be applied with more relevant results for companies of a certain size. In addition, where there are cases where fiscal and regulatory restrictions on debt are exercised, assuming fixed debt in the valuation would result in more precision. In his study, Luehrman (1997) advocates the APV method by insisting on the fact that the tax advantages of interest charges must be discounted at the cost of the debt and not at the cost of the assets. He considers debt to be a constant fraction of book value.

The criticism relating to the DCF model consists of underlining that the subjectivity of the hypotheses to be considered weakens the precision of the values obtained. Indeed, the predictions around the parameters used for the valuation of a project (or more generally of a company) are not always reliable, and this can make it less attractive than another while it may be so that the expected value may turn out to be better.

According to the DDM model, the value of the share can be considered as the present value of the expected dividends. Ohlson (1995) specifies that this value depends on accounting data that influence the assessment of the present value of expected dividends:

$$P_t = \sum_{\tau=1}^{+\infty} R_f^{-\tau} E_t[d_{t+\tau}] \quad [2.115]$$

where:

– P_t: the value of the share at date *t*;

– d_t: the dividends paid at date *t*;

– R_f: risk-free rate;

– E_t [.]: expectation of information on the date *t*.

Furthermore:

$$y_{t-1} = y_t + d_t - x_t \quad [2.116]$$

where:

– y_t: the book value of equity at date *t*;

– x_t: the benefits of the exercise t - 1 to *t*.

P_t can therefore be expressed as a function of the expected future benefits and the book values instead of expected dividends. We note as x_t^a the residual benefits at date *t*. The residual revenue x_t^a can be perceived as the decreased benefits of a charge, which constitute the use of capital. A positive residual value at t + 1 indicates a profitable period to the extent that the book rate of return x_{t+1}/y_t exceeds the cost of capital of the firm R_{f-1}. We then have:

$$x_t^a = x_t - (R_f - 1)y_{t-1} \quad [2.117]$$

Thus, residual income is defined as the difference between profits and the book value of the asset multiplied by the cost of capital. So:

$$d_t = x_t^a - y_t + R_f y_{t-1} \quad [2.118]$$

and:

$$P_t = y_t + \sum_{\tau=1}^{+\infty} R_f^{-\tau} E_t[\overline{x}_{t+\tau}^a] \quad [2.119]$$

Therefore, the value of the business is equal to its book value adjusted by the present value of expected residual income.

In order to overcome the major criticisms of the DCF method, namely how difficult it is to put into practice due to the subjectivity of the hypotheses considered, it would be interesting to investigate not an alternative method, but about how reliable these settings really are.

2.2.2.2. *Reliability of the parameters of the DCF method*

2.2.2.2.1. Measuring the variation in cash flow

Arnold and North (2008) propose a sensitivity study, which comes from the duration, in order to determine the effects of variations in expected parameters and to provide a measure of the variation in cash flows[3]. Duration corresponds to the sensitivity analysis that relates to changes in interest rates within a portfolio of bonds. This is the period at the end of which profitability is no longer affected by changes in interest rates because it appears as the discounted average lifespan of all flows (interest and capital). In other words, the duration of a financial instrument is defined as

3 The approach can also be applied at the equity level by incorporating cash flow and at the portfolio level.

the average lifespan of its financial flows weighted by their present value. So, all other elements being equal, the greater the duration, the greater the risk. According to Macaulay (1938), the duration D that generates cash flow CF is defined as the average duration of repayments of a bond (principal and interest) weighted by its present market value.

$$D = \frac{\sum_{t=1}^{n} \frac{tCF_t}{(1+i)^t}}{\sum_{t=1}^{n} \frac{CF_t}{(1+i)^t}} \quad [2.120]$$

$$D = \frac{\sum_{t=1}^{n} \frac{t\,CF_t}{(1+i)^t}}{P} \quad [2.121]$$

where:

– P: price of bond;

– *i*: discount rate.

Therefore, the duration corresponds to the average of the dates that the flows are received, weighted by the weight of each discounted cash flow in all of the flows (the fraction of each term represents the weighting coefficient). The sensitivity S of a bond expresses the relative change in percentage of the price P of a bond for a change in the interest rate i. And so:

$$S = \frac{\frac{\Delta P}{P}}{\Delta i} = \frac{1}{P}\frac{\Delta P}{\Delta i} = \frac{1}{P}\,P'(i) \quad [2.122]$$

Or:

$$P = \sum_{t=1}^{n} \frac{CF_t}{(1+t)^t} = \sum_{t=1}^{n} CF_t(1+i)^{-t} \quad [2.123]$$

Consequently:

$$S = \frac{\frac{\Delta P}{P}}{\Delta i} = -\frac{D}{1+i} \quad [2.124]$$

where:

– P: bond price;

– S: sensitivity;

– D: duration.

Duration can be used to find a variation in the bond price given a variation of the discount rate according to Bodie *et al.* (2004).

$$D = -\frac{\frac{\Delta P}{P}}{\frac{\Delta i}{(1+i)}} = -\left[\frac{\Delta P}{\Delta i}\right] \times \left[\frac{(1+i)}{P}\right] \quad [2.125]$$

$$\frac{\Delta P}{P} = -D\left[\frac{\Delta i}{(1+i)}\right] \quad [2.126]$$

The length of the duration indicates how sensitive the price of a bond is to changes in the interest rate. A longer duration means a greater change in the price of the bond as the interest rate moves. To mitigate the risk of interest rate fluctuations, several types of securities can be combined to form a target or optimal portfolio duration. Thus, the valuation of a project V equivalent to a zero-coupon bond is characterized by cash flows CF_i and the terminal value VT_N assessed over the duration of project N:

$$V = \sum_{i=0}^{N}\left[\frac{CF_i}{(1+k)^i}\right] + \frac{VT_N}{(1+k)^N} \quad [2.127]$$

$$VT_N = \frac{CF_N \times (1+g)}{(k-g)} \quad [2.128]$$

where g is the infinite growth rate assuming $k > g$.

$$V = \sum_{i=0}^{N-1}\left[\frac{CF_i}{(1+k)^i}\right] + \left[\frac{CF_N}{(1+k)^N}\right] \times \left[1 + \frac{(1+g)}{(k-g)}\right] \quad [2.129]$$

The negative partial derivative of the project cash flows relating to the discount rate gives:

$$-\frac{\Delta V}{\Delta k} = -\sum_{i=0}^{N-1}\left[-\frac{i\,CF_i}{(1+k)^{i+1}}\right] + \left[\frac{N\,CF_N}{(1+k)^{N+1}}\right] \times \left[1 + \frac{(1+g)}{(k-g)}\right] + \left[\frac{CF_N}{(1+k)^N}\right] \times \left[\frac{(1+g)}{(k-g)^2}\right] \quad [2.130]$$

$$-\frac{\Delta V}{\Delta k} = \sum_{i=0}^{N-1}\left[\frac{i\,CF_i}{(1+k)^{i+1}}\right] + \left[\frac{N\,CF_N}{(1+k)^{N+1}}\right] \times \left[1 + \frac{(1+g)}{(k-g)}\right] + \left[\frac{N\,CF_N}{(1+k)^{N+1}}\right] \times \left[\frac{(1+k)(1+g)}{N\,(k-g)^2}\right] \quad [2.131]$$

$$-\frac{\Delta V}{\Delta k} = \sum_{i=1}^{N-1}\left[\frac{i\,CF_i}{(1+k)^{i+1}}\right] + \left[\frac{N\,CF_N}{((1+k)^{N+1}}\right] \times \left[1 + \frac{(1+g)}{(k-g)} + \frac{(1+k)\times(1+g)}{N\,(k-g)^2}\right] \quad [2.132]$$

By multiplying equation [2.132] by (1 + k) and by dividing it by [2.129], we obtain the project duration:

$$D_P = \frac{\left\{\sum_{i=1}^{N-1}\left[\frac{i \times CF_i}{(1+k)^i}\right]+\left[\frac{N \times CF_N}{(1+k)^N}\right]\times\left[1+\frac{(1+g)}{(k-g)}+\frac{(1+k)\times(1+g)}{N\times(k-g)^2}\right]\right\}}{\left\{\sum_{i=0}^{N-1}\left[\frac{CF_i}{(1+k)^i}\right]+\left[\frac{CF_N}{(1+k)^N}\right]\times\left[1+\frac{(1+g)}{(k-g)}\right]\right\}} \qquad [2.133]$$

The duration of the project also varies over time if the parameters change. To enter the variation in duration as a function of the discount rate, the "convexity" of a project, C_P, is based on the second derivative of the value of the project relative to the discount rate:

$$C_P = \frac{\Delta^2 V}{\Delta k^2} \times \frac{1}{V} \qquad [2.134]$$

The greater the convexity of the project, the greater the variation in duration with a variation in the discount rate. Convexity measures the instability of duration if the discount rate is adjusted. For an infinite horizon similar to [2.129], we have:

$$C_P = \frac{\sum_{i=1}^{N-1}[i\,(i+1)CF_i]+\left[\frac{N(N+1)CF_N}{(1+k)^{N+2}}\right]\left[1+\frac{(1+g)}{(k-g)}\right]+\frac{2(1+k)(1+g)}{(N+1)(k-g)^2}+\left[\frac{2(1+k)^2(1+g)}{N(N+1)(k-g)^3}\right]}{\sum_{i=0}^{N-1}\left[\frac{CF_i}{(1+k)^i}\right]+\left[\frac{CF_N}{(1+k)^N}\right]\left[1+\frac{(1+g)}{(k-g)}\right]}$$

$$= \frac{\sum_{i=1}^{N}\left[\frac{i\times(i+1)CF_i}{(1+k)^{i+2}}\right]}{\sum_{i=0}^{N}\left[\frac{CF_i}{(1+k)^i}\right]} \qquad [2.135]$$

The concept of duration can be applied to an "internal" parameter. Also, if we take a project at time *i*, a function of the internal parameter θ influences the cash flows, CF_i (θ). The duration that relates to this parameter therefore depends exclusively on the project itself by its capacity to generate cash flows. We then see a notable difference with the analysis of the duration of the discount rate, which takes into account the cash flows as such and assesses only the effect of its own variation. Thus, equation [2.130] becomes:

$$-\frac{\Delta V}{\Delta\theta} = -\left\{\sum_{i=1}^{N}\left[\frac{\frac{\Delta CF_i(\theta)}{\Delta\theta}}{(1+k)^i}\right]\right\} \qquad [2.136]$$

The duration of the D_{PRM} project parameter gives[4]:

$$D_{PRM} = -\left[\frac{\Delta V}{\Delta \theta}\right] \times \left[\frac{1}{V}\right] \quad [2.137]$$

$$\frac{\Delta V}{V} = -[D_{PRM}] \times \Delta\theta \quad [2.138]$$

Therefore, suppose that the internal parameter of the model and the discount rate are affected by a common factor, λ, such as inflation. Respectively, [2.136], [2.137] and [2.138] become:

$$\frac{\Delta V}{\Delta\lambda} = -\left\{\sum_{i=0}^{N}\left[\frac{\frac{\Delta CF_i(\theta[\lambda])}{\Delta\theta[\lambda]} \times \frac{\Delta\theta[\lambda]}{\Delta\lambda}}{(1+k[\lambda])^i}\right] - \left[\frac{i \times CF(\theta[\lambda])_i \times \left(\frac{\Delta k[\lambda]}{\Delta\lambda}\right)}{(1+k[\lambda])^{i+1}}\right]\right\} \quad [2.139]$$

$$D_{PRM} = -\left[\frac{\Delta V}{\Delta\lambda}\right] \times \left[\frac{1}{V}\right] \quad [2.140]$$

$$\frac{\Delta V}{V} = -[D_{PRM}] \times \Delta\lambda \quad [2.141]$$

Suppose that the project ends in N years. Let us take:

– OC: operating costs;

– CL: current liabilities;

– CA: current assets;

– WCR: working capital requirement;

– FA: fixed asset;

– AMO: amortizations;

– IT_0: initial turnover;

– T: corporate tax rate.

These parameters are measured and expressed as a percentage of sales. Linear depreciation is correlated with turnover (depending on fixed assets):

4 The term (1 + k) in Macaulay's formula simplifies the calculation and is not useful for converting duration into a percentage change in price. This is the reason why the term is not introduced in equations [2.137] and [2.138].

$$V(CA) = \frac{CA_0 \times (1+g)}{(k-g)} \times \left[1 - \frac{(1+g)^N}{(1+k)^N}\right] \quad [2.142]$$

$$V(\Delta BFR) = V(CA) \times (\Delta CA - \Delta CL) \times \left[1 - \frac{1}{(1+g)}\right] \quad [2.143]$$

$$V(\Delta FA) = V(CA) \times (\Delta AI) \times \left[1 - \frac{1}{(1+g)}\right] \quad [2.144]$$

$$V(AMO) = V(CA) \times (\Delta AI) \times (\Delta AMO) \times \left[1 - \frac{1}{(1+g)}\right] \div 2 \quad [2.145]$$

$$V = \left\{\frac{CA_0(1+g)}{(k-g)} \times \left[1 - \frac{(1+g)^N}{(1+k)^N}\right]\right\} \times \left\{(1 - \Delta DE)(1 - T) + \frac{\Delta AI \times \Delta AMO\left[1 + \frac{1}{1+g}\right]}{2} \times T - \left((\Delta CA - \Delta CL + \Delta AI) \times \left[1 - \frac{1}{1+g}\right]\right)\right\} \quad [2.146]$$

To find the duration of the internal parameter relative to *g*, we include it by multiplying the derivative by (1 + g) and dividing by [2.146]. Let A = V(CA) and decompose the equation:

$$B = -\frac{\Delta A}{\Delta g} \times (1+g) = A \times \left[\frac{(1+g)}{(1+k)} - 1\right] + \frac{CA_0 \times (1+g)}{(k-g)} \times \left[\frac{N \times (1+g)^N}{(1+k)^N}\right] \quad [2.147]$$

$$C = (1 - \Delta DE) \times (1 - T) + \frac{\Delta AI \times \Delta AMO \times \left[1 + \frac{1}{(1+g)}\right]}{2} \times T \quad [2.148]$$

$$-\left((\Delta CA - \Delta CL + \Delta AI) \times \left[1 - \frac{1}{1+g}\right]\right)$$

$$D = -\frac{\Delta C}{\Delta g} \times (1+g) = \frac{\left[\frac{\Delta AI \times \Delta AMO \times T}{2} + \Delta CA - \Delta CL + \Delta AI\right]}{(1+g)} \quad [2.149]$$

$$D_{PRM} = \frac{B \times C + A \times D}{A \times C} = \left[\frac{\Delta V}{\Delta g}\right] \times \left[\frac{(1+g)}{V}\right] \quad [2.150]$$

We could add a terminal value if the project had an infinite time or even an initial cost (negative value in the denominator of [2.150]). By considering a variation of the value of the project based on the duration of the internal parameter of the project of [2.150], we get:

$$\frac{\Delta V}{V} = -D_{PRM} \times \left[\frac{\Delta g}{(1+g)}\right] \qquad [2.151]$$

2.2.2.2.2. The risk of bankruptcy: risk premium or adjusted growth rate

Shaffer (2006) proposes an extension to the DCF valuation model by considering the probability of bankruptcy[5]. Empirically, this approach relates more to forecasting premiums on equity, but it improves how risk is calibrated without penalizing the asset's value or its growth potential. It also explains the irreversible impact of the breakdown of cash flow. We might think that if the risk of bankruptcy is significant when looking only at a time distant in the future (a decade or century away), it would only be considered by a nominal proportion of investors who tend to think in years. However, a significant portion of the present value of cash flows corresponds to the terminal value. For example, assuming an annual FCF growth rate of 3% and a discount rate of 4%, it turns out that 62% of the present value is from FCF generated in more than 50 years[6]. To the extent that bankruptcy acts as a barrier that absorbs cash flow, there are interdependencies between bankruptcy risk and the valuation to be considered. In the event of bankruptcy, shareholders may receive a residual sum (after having paid off the creditors) and no longer receive continuous flows based on the returns achieved. Shaffer quantifies the impact of this absorbing barrier (which is economically important[7]) on valuation and shows that it hinders the assumption that an additional linear risk premium exists. The annual probability of bankruptcy, given as a starting point, can be empirically "benchmarked" either by historical reference of the aggregates or by obtaining specific company estimates by applying a statistical model of company bankruptcy.

---

5 Similar approaches have been put forward through bond valuation: Pye (1974) used a bankruptcy premium by calculating the expected present value of bond payments subject to a default stationary time-discrete process (Litterman and Iben 1991).

6 The proportion of the present value that results from CF beyond year T is: [(1 + g)/(1 + r)]T for the flows whose growth rate is *g* and discount rate is *r*.

7 Most of the asset value – which can be attributed to Gordon's growth model – results from expected returns in the distant future. Thus, it is intuitively plausible to think that correcting the likelihood that these returns will be terminated at some point involves a substantial reduction in the total expected value.

The analysis ignores other sources of risk, but this does not change the valuation, since the analysis does not assume that investors are risk-averse (that they require a risk premium). The analysis is general and although it could be integrated into a continuous-time model (such as that of Dufie and Singleton (1999)), Gordon's growth model is used for clarity. Remember that without default risk, the present value of future cash flows V is:

$$V = \sum_{t=0}^{\infty} \frac{c_t}{(1+k)^t} = \frac{c_0(1+k)}{k-g} \quad [2.152]$$

where:

– c_t: cash flow from assets at the start of the year *t*;

– *k*: annual discount rate;

– c_0: initial cash flow.

Cash flows are assumed to grow at the rate $g < k$. Cash flows can be dividend payments; the infinite time horizon then reflects the fact that stocks have no maturity. Then, the model incorporates the probability p ($0 < p < 1$) that the asset will default in any given year, which will cancel out subsequent cash flows. Suppose that this probability is independent of *t*, the risk of bankruptcy following a simple distribution and bankruptcy or survival being characterized by an independent series[8]. Let us also ignore the possibility that investors will receive a lump sum of liquidation payment in the event of bankruptcy. Under these assumptions, the probability of the firm going bankrupt in year T is equal to the product of p times the probability that the firm survives to year T, or $p\,(1 - p)^T$. In the absence of bankruptcy, cash flows continue to follow a non-stochastic growth rate g. The expected present value V_A of the cash flows is:

$$V_A = \frac{c_0(1+k)(1-p)}{k+p-g(1-p)} \quad [2.153]$$

where the denominator is greater than that of equation [2.152] for all $p > 0$ and is therefore strictly positive when $r > g$ (as required by Gordon's basic growth model). Equation [2.153] corresponds to the valuation of an asset with an initial cash flow c_0, which increases at an annual rate *g*, discounted at

8 The model can be extended to reflect more general bankruptcy processes, as in the Duffie and Singleton bond analysis.

an annual rate k, subject to an annual probability of failure p (or maturity, or default irreversible). Equation [2.153] also corresponds to equation [2.152] if $p = 0$. In other words, Gordon's valuation of growth without failure is a special case of valuation with a risk of stochastic bankruptcy.

Note that by "correcting" equation [2.152] based on the probability of failure without taking into account the permanent cessation of cash flows in the event of bankruptcy, the annual cash flows per period are replaced by c_t $(1 - p)$. We then have $\frac{c_0 (1 + k) (1 - p)}{(k-g)}$. The numerator is the same as equation [2.153], but the denominator is always smaller, which means that the valuation is greater than the correct calculation of equation [2.153]. And so, this is consistent with the difference between permanent bankruptcy and uncorrelated annual shortcomings.

This valuation model applied to equity can also be used when valuing the company itself. The main difference is the structure of debt and equity, which affects both the probability of insolvency in each period and the net asset value at the time of bankruptcy. When a company goes bankrupt, it results in losses being incurred by both shareholders and creditors. In addition, liquidation costs are added to the establishment undergoing the liquidation procedure. A comprehensive model of company value must therefore be distinct from the equity valuation model, precisely because of these expected bankruptcy costs. In this case, a comparative analysis is carried out between the assumed liquidation costs and aggregate net worth at the time of bankruptcy. Thus, equation [2.153] can be applied to a firm facing difficulties, but not necessarily in bankruptcy. Such a company is likely to make no gain and pay no dividend – i.e. a situation wherein DCFs are known to provide poor valuations. Severely troubled companies with negative bottom lines do not need to claim a model to identify their difficult situation, and at the time of bankruptcy, the relevant calculation is the present net asset value rather than the risk-adjusted projection of future value. The most useful application of this model therefore concerns companies with a moderate risk of bankruptcy. The impact of low bankruptcy probabilities on the valuation of risk premiums is considerably greater than previously recognized. Thus, taking into account the impact of such a risk is important for all companies. Equation [2.153] can also be used to calculate the ratio of the value of the asset to the current flows generated

($V_{asset} = V_A/c_0$), which would be consistent with the particular values that *k*, *g* and *p* take, assuming a neutral risk:

$$\frac{\partial V_{asset}}{\partial g} = \frac{(1+k)(1-p)^2}{D^2} > 0 \qquad [2.154]$$

$$\frac{\partial V_{asset}}{\partial k} = \frac{(1+g)(1-p)^2}{D^2} < 0 \qquad [2.155]$$

$$\frac{\partial V_{asset}}{\partial p} = \frac{(1+k)^2}{D^2} < 0 \qquad [2.156]$$

where $D = g(p-1) + p + k$, which corresponds to the denominator $k - g$ of equation [2.152], plus an adjustment for the effect of bankruptcy risk at any time, namely $p(1 + g)$. The *price-to-dividend* ratio increases with the expected growth rate but decreases with the discount rate and the annual probability of bankruptcy. Note that *g* and *p* enter equation [2.153]. This functional formula makes us question whether an additional risk premium or a growth adjustment is sufficient to reflect the impact of the probability of bankruptcy on the valuation of an asset. Consider the convexity of V_{asset} with respect to *p* characterized by:

$$\frac{\partial^2 V_{asset}}{\partial p^2} = \frac{2(1+g)(1+k)^2}{D^3} < 0 \qquad [2.157]$$

where the sign is established because $D > (r - g) > 0$. And so, the price-to-dividend ratio is strictly convex at *p*. Combined with equation [2.154], equation [2.157] establishes that the marginal decrease of V_{asset} weakens as the values of *p* increase.

In the DCF method, the integration of risk corresponds either to a downward adjustment of the growth rate used or as an additional constant (risk premium) in the process of discounting. These additional values are used not only to estimate the assets but also to calculate the returns from a given risk profile or, conversely, to deduce the levels of risk involved by the observed asset returns. Therefore, although equation [2.153] is suitable for practical applications, it is necessary to combine equation [2.152] with equation [2.153] if we want to consider an adjusted growth rate G or a premium additional risk R.

To find the expression for the adjusted growth rate of cash flows that incorporates the probability of bankruptcy in the valuation provided by Gordon's model, *k* is fixed:

$$\frac{c_0(1+k)}{k-G} = \frac{c_0(1+k)(1-p)}{k+p-g(1-p)} > 0 \qquad [2.158]$$

$$G = \frac{g-p(1+k)}{1-p} \qquad [2.159]$$

The downward adjustment of the growth rate to be attributed to the risk of bankruptcy is equal to a period of anticipation of the future value of the risk rate (the ratio of the annual probability of bankruptcy to the annual probability of survival): $G < g$ for all $p \in (0,1)$ and for $k \geq 0$. Moreover, $G \rightarrow g$ for $p \rightarrow 0$.

We can note that G is linear in *g* (with $\frac{\partial G}{\partial g} = 1$), requiring only one additional term to correct the risk of bankruptcy. The adjustment factor is nonlinear *k* and *p*. We thus have:

$$\frac{\partial G}{\partial p} = -\frac{1+k}{(1-p)^2} < 0 \qquad [2.160]$$

$$\frac{\partial G}{\partial k} = -\frac{p}{(1-p)} < 0 \qquad [2.161]$$

Thus, a greater probability of bankruptcy reduces the effective growth rate of returns (see equation [2.160]). And a larger discount rate combines the impact of the risk of bankruptcy on net present value by reducing the effective growth rate (see equation [2.161]). The concavity of G with respect to *p* can also be evaluated:

$$\frac{\partial^2 G}{\partial p^2} = \frac{2(1+k)}{(1-p)^3} < 0 \qquad [2.162]$$

And so G is strictly concave at *p*. Combined with equation [2.160], this result establishes that the downward adjustment of G is greater as the values of *p* increase.

As an alternative to adjusting the assumed growth rate of cash flows, an additional risk premium R can be calculated to incorporate the risk of bankruptcy. Following this approach, we solve the following equation in order to define the conventional valuation that corresponds to the corrected valuation for the risk of bankruptcy in equation [2.153]:

$$\frac{c_0(1+k+R)}{k-G-g} = \frac{c_0(1+k)(1-p)}{k+p-g(1-p)} \qquad [2.163]$$

$$R = \frac{p(1-r)^2}{1+g-p(k+g+2)} \qquad [2.164]$$

where the denominator is different from zero for all $p \neq (1+g)/(k+g+2)$. The risk premium is a function of risk-free rate, the growth rate and the probability of failure. By defining E, the denominator of equation [2.164] which corresponds to the basic crude growth rate, $1 + g$, minus an adjustment for the effect of bankruptcy risk over time, $p(k+g+2)$, we find:

$$\frac{\partial R}{\partial g} = \frac{p(1-p)(1+k)^2}{E^3} < 0 \qquad [2.165]$$

$$\frac{\partial R}{\partial p} = \frac{(1+g)(1+k)^2}{E^2} > 0 \qquad [2.166]$$

$$\frac{\partial R}{\partial k} = \frac{p(1+k)[p(k+3)-2-2g(1-p)]}{E^2} \qquad [2.167]$$

where equation [2.167] < 0 if $p < 2/3$ when r and g are very small positive numbers. $R > 0$, for a sufficiently small p, although $p > ½$ can result in $R < 0$. $R \rightarrow 0$ and $p \rightarrow 0$. The close correspondence between the risk premium model given historical bankruptcy rates and market risk premiums observed during the same period suggests another use of the model. Given the values of *k* and *g*, equation [2.164] can be solved for p as a function of the observed risk premium on the equity of a particular firm. If the market risk premiums correctly reflect the risk of bankruptcy, the implied value of *p* provides a convenient way to summarize information about this risk embedded in the market price of the company's shares:

$$p = \frac{R(1+g)}{(1+k)^2+R(k+g+2)} \qquad [2.168]$$

The model can be extended to calculate the stock value of a company whose growth rate changes drastically. Cash flows after this transition would either remain at the level observed before the period or increase at a different rate. For example, a company has a phase of rapid initial growth, followed by a downturn phase. If the company's cash flows grow at a rate *g* until period T and then remain constant thereafter, the present value of the cash flows if $0 \leq g < k$ is:

$$\begin{aligned} V_{A_T} &= \sum_{t=0}^{T} \frac{c_0(1+g)^t}{(1+k)^t} + \sum_{t=T+1}^{\infty} \frac{c_0(1+g)^T}{(1+k)^t} \\ &= \left[\frac{c_0}{(1+k)^T}\right]\left[\frac{(1+k)^{T+1}-(1+g)^{T+1}}{(k-g)+\frac{(1+g)^T}{k}}\right] \end{aligned} \quad [2.169]$$

If the transition occurs with the probability *p* during a period *t*, then the value of equity that corresponds to the value of discounted cash flows is:

$$V = \sum_{T=0}^{\infty} p(1-p)^T V_{A_T} = \left[\frac{c_0(1+k)(k+p)}{k(k+p-g+pg)}\right] \quad [2.170]$$

Equation [2.170] is a return to the Gordon valuation, $c_o(1 + k)/(k - g)$, as a special case if $p = 0$. We may also consider either an additional risk premium or an equivalent constant growth rate to adjust the valuation to be equal to this expression. The effective discount rate R (k + additional risk premium), to define $c_o (1 + R)/(R - g)$ equal to equation [2.170], can be calculated as follows:

$$R = \frac{g[p(1+2k)+k^2]+k(k+p)}{kg(1-p)+k+p} \quad [2.171]$$

We can calculate an equivalent constant growth rate G leading to the same valuation while discounting at the risk-free rate by $c_o(1 + k)/(k - G)$:

$$G = \frac{kg(1-p)}{k+p} \quad [2.172]$$

Therefore, if a firm's cash flows show a stochastic transition from positive growth at rate *g* to a zero growth rate, the valuation of these cash flows is given by equation [2.170]; the same valuation can be obtained by substituting either R from equation [2.171] or G from equation [2.172] to the Gordon growth model. This analysis can be generalized in the case of positive growth after period T but at a different rate γ. The present value of the cash flows is:

$$V_{A_T} = \sum_{t=0}^{T} \frac{c_0(1+g)^t}{(1+k)^t} + \sum_{t=T+1}^{\infty} \frac{c_0(1+g)^T(1+\gamma)^{t-T}}{(1+k)^t}$$

$$= \left[\frac{c_0}{(1+k)^T}\right] \times \left[\frac{(1+k)^{T+1}-(1+g)^{T+1}}{k-g} + \frac{(1+g)^T(1+\gamma)}{k-\gamma}\right] \quad [2.173]$$

If $0 \leq g < k$, the expression reduces equation [2.169] to a special case if $\gamma = 0$.

With a transition probability of the growth rate g to γ, the present value associated with equation [2.173] can be calculated analogously to equation [2.170]:

$$V = \frac{c_0(1+r)}{r-g} + c_0 p(1+r) \times \frac{\frac{1+\gamma}{r-\gamma} - \frac{1+g}{r-g}}{r-g+p+pg} \quad [2.174]$$

which reduces equation [2.152] if $p = 0$ or $\gamma = g$ and equation [2.170] if $\gamma = 0$. The adjusted discount rate (or growth rate) to obtain the same valuation using Gordon's growth model is:

$$R = \frac{g[p(1+2k)+k^2]+k(k+p)}{kg(1-p)+k+p} \quad [2.175]$$

$$G = \frac{g(1-p)(\gamma-r)-\gamma p(1+r)}{\gamma(1-p)-r-p} \quad [2.176]$$

And these expressions reduce, respectively, equations [2.171] and [2.172] for $\gamma = 0$. Therefore, if a company's cash flows show a stochastic transition from one growth rate to another, the valuation of these cash flows is given by equation [2.174]; the same valuation can be obtained by substituting either R from equation [2.175] or G from equation [2.176] to the Gordon growth model.

Consequently, this analysis justifies the use of either the growth adjustment or an additional risk premium and demonstrates the responsiveness of these two terms to three exogenous factors (risk-free rate, expected growth rate of cash flows and probability of periodic failure).

Reviews in the literature are focused on theoretical adjustments vis-à-vis optimizing the financial structure and beyond this, on valuation methods by discounting cash flows – adjustments based on conceptual parameters. It therefore seems interesting to analyze studies that address the performance of valuation methods according to specific contexts. Indeed, certain methods could prove to be more appropriate to the detriment of others when it comes to valuing a transaction with leverage or a company with particular characteristics in terms of structure, size, type of activity or the particular stage of its development.

2.3. Contextual impacts and adjustments

Kaplan and Ruback (1995) compare performance in terms of market anticipation according to different valuation methods, based on the APV method and on the EBITDA multiple, from a sample of companies that have undergone management buyout operations and recapitalizations. In this context, they recommend retaining a high risk premium and generally favoring discounting cash flow methods.

By focusing on the sector multiples method, Lie and Lie (2002) find that overall the asset multiple provides better estimates and that the EBITDA multiple provides better estimates than the EBIT multiple. In other words, allocations and takeovers would adversely affect the enterprise value. Alford (1992) carries out an important study about samples and variety of tests. He concludes that the P/E multiple provides more precision when benchmarks are chosen on the basis of industry and when businesses classified as such have similar financial returns and asset values. It is in this sense that Zarowin (1990) and Kim and Ratter (1999) extend their research on the performance of the P/E multiple according to different contexts.

Hotchkiss and Mooradian (1998) focus on company takeovers in the situation of bankruptcy. According to them, the prices paid, which are calculated from the revenue or asset multiple, are on average 45% lower than the corresponding transactions between companies operating in the same industry that are in good health. In other words, the two researchers believe that this result comes from the information imbalance that exists in such situations. Gilson *et al.* (2000) compare the market value for shares of listed companies that are restructured after a situation of bankruptcy with their discounted cash flow valuations which are calculated from their reorganization plans. Significant disparities can be noted depending on the time that has elapsed since the restructuring. If the valuations do not correspond to reality, these differences are not, according to the researchers, linked to errors in calculation. Rather, they are due to problems that relate to the quality of information that is available during the administrative process that has been initiated in order to declare the situation of bankruptcy (replacing the market). Along with this, they are due to strategic biases, namely agency conflicts, which benefit certain parties such as creditors or management when the value is underestimated. In this context, valuation is used more for strategic purposes and becomes a determining element in negotiations.

Damodaran (2009) tries to propose an appropriate method to value a young company. He affirms that valuation must be linked to sales or to the net result, incorporate a target rate of return and focus on short-term forecasts (2–5 years of business plans, coinciding with the resale forecast for the benefit of a venture capital fund).

2.3.1. *Leverage transactions*

The principle of leverage buy out (LBO) consists of acquiring a target company by an *ad hoc* takeover holding company that is financed in large part by debt. The equity of the holding company alone represents a lower investment than that which would have been necessary to buy shares of the target company. The leverage effect can thus be put into practice by considering that the financial profitability of the target is greater than the cost of the debt. The holding's acquisition debt is then repaid thanks to dividends that are paid by the target and, to a lesser extent, thanks to the cash generated by the exit from the LBO. For the latter to work, it is necessary for the target to operate in a mature market that is synonymous with moderate investments, thus facilitating the payment of dividends. The latter is also a function of the target's debt level, which at a reasonable level allows it to allocate most of its cash to the takeover holding company.

In addition, it is recommended that visibility is as clear as possible, as this will make the business plan and forecasts more reliable when it comes to the exit of the investment funds when the target is introduced to the stock market or it is sold to an industry or to another fund. Initially, the sale price of the target is capped at the maximum amount of finance likely to be raised by the takeover holding company. Therefore, the value of the target is no longer an assumption but an outcome. It corresponds to the maximum amount of funds that can feasibly be raised by the takeover holding company in the form of capital, subscribed by the investment fund(s) and the acquisition debt raised from banks. In fact, determining the value of the target means structuring the financing of the holding company. Acquisition debt, for its part, is directly linked to the expected profitability of the target. It is adjusted by incorporating the idea that repayment will take place over a period of 7–9 years through the dividends distributed by the target to the holding company. The profit distribution rate of the target is assumed to be 100% as soon as the LBO is set up. In addition, the debt is calibrated so that the holding company maintains a cash flow that is in slight excess, so as not to generate additional financing needs. Finally, it is necessary to respect financial ratios or covenants that allow lending institutions and financial bodies to control the progress of the LBO. Equity is set at a level which ensures that investment funds receive an internal rate of return of about 20–30% in 3 years. This is on the assumption that the fund will exit by IPO, by a sale to an industry, or to another fund on the basis of a multiple of EBITDA or EBIT, according to market conditions at the time of setting up the LBO. The value of the target is, in practice, slightly lower than the sum of the values of the shareholders' equity and the debt of the holding company, because the latter must also finance various costs of about 3–4% of the holding value of the transaction (fees for lawyers, advice, legal, accounting and tax audits and payment of a commitment commission on the acquisition debt), which are all linked to the process of acquisition.

Kaplan and Ruback (1995) attempt to compare the market value of a sample of 51 characteristic management buyout and recapitalization transactions with valuation methods based on discounting cash flows using the APV method (adjusted present value) and on the EBITDA multiple (thus excluding the P/E multiple due to the fact that companies have different financial structures). The empirical problem of their study is to understand whether the parametric assumptions of the APV methods specific to the company having undergone these types of leveraged transactions provide better results than the incorporation of expectations that are contained within the comparables methods. Their work therefore begins with the definition of different valuation models using the APV method initially developed by Myers (1974). They consider three different weighted average costs of capital distinguished in this by their respective beta: the first is calculated from the beta of the company, the second from the sector beta and the third from the market beta (this is that of the sample). In addition to trying to compare the valuation details of these same cash flow discounting methods, they also want to make comparisons with estimates based on the EBITDA multiple. Likewise, they define three comparables methods: the first based on a benchmark of comparable companies, the second resulting from comparable transactions and the third resulting from transactions that have been carried out in the same industry between comparable companies.

The median – derived from APV company valuations based on the company beta – is 6% above the trade value. Therefore, we see that valuations using the beta of the sample (market) are closest to the transaction values in terms of both median and mean. We can also see that the standard deviation is the smallest, which is proof that the variations are smaller with this method. Regarding the multiples method, in view of the median, we would recommend *a priori* to use an EBITDA multiple from a sample of comparable transactions between companies in the same industry. However, by analyzing its standard deviation, we note that this type of sample provides the most disparate values. Moreover, Kaplan and Ritter express that the number of companies that combine these two criteria and therefore constitute this type of sample is limited. Indeed, 13 of the 51 companies in the overall sample could not be grouped together in a repository. We can therefore suspect that it is difficult, if not impossible, depending on the period and sector of activity, to constitute this type of sample in practice. The work of the two researchers can be extended by presenting the error estimates as a function of the risk premiums applied.

	Methods based on different WACCs			**Methods based on different samples**		
	Company beta	**Sector beta**	**Market beta**	**Comparable companies**	**Comparable transactions**	**Comparable transactions between comparable companies**
Median	6%	6.2%	2.5%	-18.1%	5.9%	-0.1%
Average	8%	7.1%	3.1%	-16.6%	0.3%	-0.7%
Standard deviation	28.1%	25.1%	22.6%	25.4%	22.3%	28.7%
Median beta	0.81	0.84	0.91			

Table 2.2. *Errors (the definition of the error results from the calculation* $\left(\frac{Estimated\ value}{Transaction\ value}\right)$*) between the values of the transactions carried out and those of the different valuation models*

	Methods based on different WACCs			Methods based on different samples		
Median risk premiums	**Company beta**	**Sector beta**	**Market beta**	**Comparable companies**	**Comparable transactions**	**Comparable transactions between comparable companies**
5%	25%	24.8%	21.2%	30.1%	29.2%	26.6%
6%	16.4%	17.7%	13.6%	25.2%	23%	20.3%
9%	-2.3%	-3.1%	-7.6%	20.3%	17%	17.4%

Table 2.3. *Variation in valuation errors depending on the size of risk premiums applied to the different valuation methods*

The results indicate that it makes good sense to use a high risk premium to obtain a more accurate valuation. For example, with the APV method based on the beta of the company, applying a risk premium of 6%, the median of the valuation error is of the order of 16.5%, while when the premium of risk is 9%, the median indicates that the valuation underestimates the value of the transaction actually carried out by only 2.3%[15]. To refine their analysis, Kaplan and Ritter present error histograms for each method. They find that APV methods based on an industry or market beta show a greater tendency to provide valuations below 15% error, while methods based on the EBITDA multiple give more uniform results. In other words, about 60% of the valuations carried out by one of the two APV methods mentioned above are less than 15% of the value of the transaction carried out, while the percentage of the valuations resulting from the multiple of EBITDA based on a benchmark of comparable companies or transactions – for this same criterion of precision regarding the value of the (i.e. 15%) – relate to 37 and 47% of the valuations, respectively[16]. Therefore, Kaplan and Ruback favor discounted cash flow methods for three reasons.

15 The risk premium that is calculated by the two researchers and used in the analysis is equal to 7.42%.

16 The valuations carried out using the EBITDA multiple method from a benchmark of similar transactions for the same sector of activity are 58% below 15% of the value of the transaction. One would tend therefore to claim that they provide results that are similar to those obtained by the APV-based valuations. However, if this turns out to be true theoretically, for the reasons mentioned above, namely the difficulty inherent in putting them into practice, any analysis that legitimizes their interest will be excluded.

They tend to provide more valuations below 15% accuracy. In addition, the two best comparables methods studied here use transaction repositories, and in practice, their scope is far too small, unlike the discounted cash flow methods. Finally, they estimate their prediction of perfectible cash flow, and therefore, in practice, the financial bodies with more information can adjust the valuations more effectively using this type of method.

Even though, in theory, the most precise valuation of the company is part of a medium- and long-term development perspective, i.e. by applying the DCF method, in practice, it can be found to be biased and unreliable. Indeed, it may be difficult depending on the context, to accurately anticipate future flows and/or to assess a discount rate that takes into account the optimal amount of risk. This is the reason why analysts and investment bankers may prefer to use – or at least provide in addition – a valuation based on the market comparables method. Also, it seems interesting to ask if empirically there may or may not be a multiple that provides more precision around the value of the company in absolute terms, depending on a specific context or market sector.

2.3.2. *Stock market multiples: from the impact of structures to anticipating profitability*

Amir and Lev (1996) study valuations in the telecommunications industry and show that the first factor that impacts enterprise value is the population of a franchise territory and not financial variables. Thus, there is no answer as to which multiple should be favored over another: the relevance of the value that comes from the P/E can be as well established as that found from the asset multiple. Thinking more globally, Lie and Lie (2002) constitute a sample of more than 8,600 companies that they value using 10 different multiples. Then, they estimate the errors between their calculations and the market values. Among the multiples based on enterprise value and observing the percentage of valuations below 15% of errors compared to the market value, it turns out that the multiple of assets provides the best estimate (35%) and the multiple of turnover the least precise estimate (23%). Moreover, from the same perspective, the multiple of P/E based on forecast results is more precise than when it is calculated from book values, according to the conclusions of Kim and Ritter (1999) developed below. In addition, the EBITDA multiple provides better estimates than the EBIT multiple. Thus, it appears that allocations and operating reversals distort value, as depreciation schedules do not accurately reflect deterioration in asset value.

Lie and Lie then separate financial corporations from non-financial corporations and analyze them. This choice of creating two separate samples is justified by the liquid asset nature of the assets of financial corporations, which facilitates evaluation compared to non-financial corporations. In line with the findings of Alford (1992) below, valuations of non-financial firms are more accurate when their size is substantial. Indeed, the smallest companies have more erratic results, while the large structures can be considered as a large portfolio of projects. In addition, regardless of the size of the structure, the multiple that confers the most faithful value to that which relates to the market is the assets multiple, and the one that confers the least is the turnover multiple. For example, Lie and Lie find that within a sample of medium-sized companies (the book value of assets ranging from $100 million to $1 billion), the valuations derived from the revenue multiple are 20% below the 15% error, compared to the market value when looking at this same criterion, the valuations that result from the assets multiple are at 30%. The dominance of the asset multiple is all the more obvious for company valuations with low (or even negative) EBITDA, relative to the book value of their assets. For companies with significant EBITDA compared to the book value of their assets, how precise the different multiples are related to whether it is P/E, asset multiple, EBITDA or EBIT; valuations located at less than 15% of the market value are about 25%. The performance of the asset multiple over other multiples becomes most pronounced when it comes to studying financial companies. The median valuation error underestimates the market values of major financial companies by 1% (the book value of assets is greater than $1 billion), and 83% of these valuations are within 15% error relative to market value.

Apart from the distinction made between non-financial and financial corporations, the Lie and Lie study does not look at specific contexts. Milicevic (2009) even shows that if in practice in order to compose their sample, investment analysts and bankers consider companies that are in the same sector of activity, they will always reside within the same branch of activity, albeit in different classification systems. In addition, the incorporation of foreign companies that follow different accounting and regulatory rules generates inaccuracies with regard to forgetting that some companies operate in different sectors, which alters a representative identification of the benchmark. In addition, the theoretical justification that companies in the same sector should have similar rates of profitability, growth and risk profiles weakens the credibility of the results obtained. Milicevic also mentions limitations faced by the transaction multiples method. Numbers provided within the same sector in a limited space-time turn out to be rather concise, while not providing satisfactory statistical data for analysis each time. In addition, market conditions are constantly changing, which can discredit the premiums for transactions that are selected for valuation. It is then a question of knowing how to identify a suitable sector of activity and understand what is the ideal size of a repository. After defining them, we must ask ourselves whether they meet the comparison conditions as such, or whether it makes sense to make certain adjustments.

It is in this sense that the empirical work of Alford (1992) attempts to detect a level of consistency when determining the benchmark of companies when the valuation is carried out by the P/E multiple. Even though Boatsman and Baskin (1981) and then LeClair (1990) had carried out empirical studies on this subject before him, the fact remains that their tests had certain methodological limitations. In fact, for their P/E test, Boatsman and Baskin used two kinds of sample for comparable companies: one based on companies that belong to the same sector of activity and the other on companies that belong to the same sector of activity with similar 10-year earning growth rates. The conclusion of their analysis leads us to consider that composing a sample of companies on the basis of the criteria of the second benchmark provides makes the valuation more precise. However, the two researchers focused on examining 80 companies over a year based only on the assessment of a single comparable company. LeClair, for his part, tests the P/E multiple with a sample of 1,165 companies that are comparable in terms of industry. He classifies them into three subsets, distinguishing them by criteria that relate to their net results (which are all positive). We thus can find a repository of companies whose results for the previous year were similar, a benchmark of companies whose average profits over 2 years are of the same type of magnitude and a benchmark of companies whose share of profits that are related to tangible and intangible assets is substantially similar. LeClair considers a different discount rate for each source of earnings. He concludes that the sample of companies with similar 2-year average net results provides the most accurate value, yet he does not test to see how the significance in the precision of the three measures is different.

Alford's influence lies in the breadth of his study. He carried out these tests on 4,698 companies in three different years (1978, 1982 and 1986) by constituting seven benchmarks which are made up of company multiples[17] that belong to various sectors of activity. He therefore studied – in addition to the criteria linked to industrial comparisons as such – potential valuation convergences between companies that only have equivalent asset values and/or financial returns. Therefore, he examines seven potential sets of comparable businesses:

– the companies that constitute the whole of the sample, i.e. the market of the companies studied;

– companies that belong to the same sector of activity that it defines using the standardized classification of American industries[18];

– companies in the sample with similar asset values;

– companies in the sample with close financial returns;

– the combination of companies that belong to the same sector of activity and have a similar asset value;

– the combination of companies that belong to the same sector of activity and which have close financial profitability;

– companies that have both an asset value and a similar financial profitability (without being from the same sector of activity).

The methodology is as follows: after having designed seven subsets, each company is valued by multiplying net income by the "categorical" P/E, which is then calculated. The "absolute prediction error", $e_{i,t}$, is then estimated, which is equal to:

$$\left| e_{i,t} = \frac{p_{i,t} - p_{i,t}}{p_{i,t}} \right| \qquad [2.177]$$

17 For example, the benchmarks for "business sectors" are made up on average of 18 companies (average of the median values over 3 years).

18 SIC: Standard Industrial Classification. Alford considers two companies to be in the same industry when they have the first three digits of their SIC code in common.

where:

– $P_{i,t}$: value of share i found by the multiple P/E method at time t;

– $p_{i,t}$: current (real) value of share i at time t.

Finally, the mean of the median values is measured for the absolute prediction errors[19] for each subset. It is then concluded that the P/E tends to be more precise when comparable companies are chosen on:

– the basis of their sector of activity. In this case, the mean of the median values for the absolute prediction errors is 24.5%;

– the combination, to a lesser extent, of the business sector with similar financial returns. In this case, the mean of the median values for absolute prediction error is 25.3%.

Alford's findings confirm a financial reality. It seems theoretically obvious that the financial profitability of the companies that make up the sample and that of the target must be of the same order of magnitude. Indeed, by multiplying the sector P/E by the net income of the company to be valued, we can obtain an estimate of potential market capitalization where:

$$\mathrm{CB} = \text{sector P/E} \,.\, \mathrm{NR} \quad [2.178]$$

$$\mathrm{CB} = \text{sector P/E}\,[(\mathrm{EBIT} - \mathrm{iD})(1 - \mathrm{t})] \quad [2.179]$$

$$\mathrm{CB} = \text{sector P/E}\,[\mathrm{EBIT}(1 - \mathrm{t}) - \mathrm{iD}(1 - \mathrm{t})] \quad [2.180]$$

$$\mathrm{CB} = \text{sector P/E}\,[\mathrm{EBIT}(1 - \mathrm{t})] - \text{sector P/E}\,[\mathrm{iD}(1 - \mathrm{t})] \quad [2.181]$$

where:

– MC: market capitalization of the company being valuated;

– NR: net result of the company being valuated;

– EBIT: operating result of the company being valuated;

– i: cost of the net debt of the company being valuated;

19 The average results from the fact that there are 3 years of data.

– D: net debt of the company being valuated;

– t: corporate tax rate.

Consequently, the sector $P/E\,[EBIT(1-t)]$ would represent the enterprise value and the sector $P/E\,[iD(1-t)]$ would represent net debt. In practice, this equality is fair if and only if:

$$D = \text{sector } P/E\,[iD(1-t)] \quad [2.182]$$

$$\text{Sector } P/E = \frac{D}{iD(1-t)} \quad [2.183]$$

$$\frac{1}{\text{Sector } P/E} = i(1-t) \quad [2.184]$$

We also know that:

$$\frac{1}{\text{Sector } P/E} = \frac{\text{Net result}}{\text{Equity}} = Rf \quad [2.185]$$

So:

$$Rf = i(1-t) \quad [2.186]$$

where Rf is the sector financial profitability.

In other words, if theoretically it seems wise to value a company by applying the sector PER to its net profit, the use of this method in practice implies that in order to achieve a greater degree of accuracy, the companies within the sector of activity have almost identical financial returns. Indeed, if the sectoral financial profitability is greater than the cost of the after-tax debt of the company to be valued, the latter's equity would be overvalued because the debt would be undervalued, and vice versa, if the sectoral financial profitability is lower than the after-tax cost of debt of the company to be valued, equity would be undervalued because the debt would be overstated. In accordance with the Dupont de Nemours formula[20], this difference in profitability can be explained through a differential in the net margin rate, the asset turnover rate and/or the use of leverage.

20 Decomposition of the financial profitability proposed by this company before World War II.

When a company's stock market status is constant, so is the P/E[21]. Indeed, it would seem *a priori* that if the stock price increases, the P/E in turn increases, but this would mean that we are forgetting that it is because, going upwards, the profit per share increases such that the market passes this expectation onto the price of the stock exchange. It is in this sense that the work of Zarowin (1990) responds empirically, using a sample of 175 companies, to the possible factor(s) that impact(s) the P/E. His study spans 5 years (from 1964 to 1968 inclusive). The companies are chosen so that their whole more or less replicates the market. To do this, he relies on an annual average beta that ranges from a minimum of 0.988 to a maximum of 1.054. He then defines two kinds of P/E[22]: the first is based on an observed benefit and the second on a "normalized" profit. The latter results from the incorporation of forecasted growth rate and risk according to the model of Litzenberger and Rao (1971). Thus, the second P/E seeks to ignore any cyclical accounting adjustments and optimizations. Zarowin then sets up 15 portfolios of companies of the same size. Classification is carried out on the basis of similar P/E. He then observes, for each year, the correlation that arises from the 15 portfolios by studying the P/E variations. He finds that the P/E correlations between the different portfolios each year are strong (close to 1) regardless of whether they are observed or normalized P/E. The results run counter to the conclusions developed by Beaver and Morse (1978), for whom variations in P/E are essentially justified by variations in accounting methods that result from considering inventory valuation rules or from taking into account the level of depreciation. Indeed, according to Zarowin's results, if the differences between the accounting methods had been the main cause of the differences in the values of P/E over time, their failure to take them into account – i.e. to consider a normalized P/E normalized "freed" from accounting constraints – should have resulted in more decorrelation (close to 0).

Zarowin completes his study by reconciling the normalized and observed P/E through regression calculations. The average of the correlation coefficients established over the years of study is 0.85, which indicates that the accounting methods are at most responsible for the variations in current P/E at 15% on average. To justify variations in P/E, Zarowin performs regression calculations between short-term and long-term forecasted growth,

21 The P/E of a company varies when it changes sector of activity.

22 He studies, more precisely, the "price-earnings ratio (P/E)", which corresponds to the reverse P/E.

beta and observed P/E. He notes that the long-term forecasted growth justifies 70% of the P/E realized, while the average coefficient of long-term forecast growth is six times greater than the growth coefficient that is actually achieved. According to him, the explanation is that the long-term growth forecasts are influenced by the observed P/E and not the other way around, namely that the multiple is affected by any forecast growth. Moreover, Zarowin's point is confirmed when he presents the correlations of the long-term forecasted growth rates of the samples across the years of study. They turn out to be close to 1. An interesting conclusion that can be deduced from this work is the non-significance of the beta, whereas the risk associated with the growth forecasts seems to be a second factor that could affect the P/E. The average correlation between beta and predicted long-term growth is 0.58. These results are in line with the tests undertaken by Tinic and West (1984) on the equilibrium model of financial assets and with those of Liu and Ziebart (1994), who examine the transversality of the variabilities of PER[23]. They uncover a significant relationship between this ratio and growth, dividend payout and company size. On the other hand, they also emphatically perceive that there is no relation between the PER and systematic risk. To complete this analysis, it would be interesting to identify the specific risk factors used by the market and to test, finally, the impact of interest rates on the P/E.

By adjusting its benchmark as Alford did, the reliability of the P/E cannot justify all valuations. In accordance with what has been developed previously, it is so to speak weak to rely on this single multiple to valuate, for example, a company that wishes to introduce its capital on the stock market. Indeed, in this case, the financial structure of the company varies appreciably from that of the companies already listed, which operate in the same sector without taking into account that their respective value of the assets is appreciably different – fundraising that can justify the IPO. In addition, when evaluating a company that wishes to make all or part of its capital public, the DCF method can definitely be ruled out because it is too imprecise. Predicting future cash flows involved may be too difficult, if not impossible to do. If we refer to the work of Varaiya *et al.* (1997), during a stock market listing, it would be necessary to recommend the use of the multiples method on the basis of accounting information. However, the work of Kim and Ratter (1999) – which aims to provide empirical evidence for the accuracy of multiples in when valuating an IPO company – suggests that,

23 They study the E/P ratio or the earning-price ratio.

without adjustments, there are too many inaccuracies when we rely solely on historical accounting data. They justify these valuation errors by asserting that listed companies in the same industry have such variable P/E relative to each other that, on that basis, any price can be justified. On the other hand, they suggest that by turning to forecast earnings (to which a growth rate and profitability rate are applied) in order to calculate the P/E, the accuracy of the valuation would improve significantly. They decide to extend their study to other multiples: market value over book value of equity, stock market price over turnover, enterprise value over turnover and enterprise value over operating cash flow. To carry out their research, they make up two repositories of 190 companies that have gone public less than a year after the announcement of their preliminary offer price. The first groups together all recent IPOs from the same industry[24] and whose data is only accounting and historical. The second brings together IPOs of comparable companies that have been chosen by classifying a company that specializes in IPO valuation[25]. In this second sample, notably, the data is forecast.

Multiples	Absolute prediction error		Percent regression of valuations included at least 15% of the current multiple	
	Mean	Median	Offer price	First quotation at close
P/E	56.5%	49.9%	14.2%	17.4%
Market value/book value of equity	33.1%	30.6%	27.4%	22.1%
Stock market price/turnover	62.4%	51.5%	13.2%	12.0%

Table 2.4. *Error between current values of multiples and predicted values of multiples according to the criteria of the first repository (accounting data)*

In the best-case scenario, when using a valuation by the multiple of the market value of equity over its book value, approximately 27% of the offer price valuations are less than 15% of the actual traded value. This same method overestimates the transaction value by an average of 33.1%. In

24 Kim and Ritter consider that two companies belong to the same industry when their SIC code is composed of four digits.

25 Renaissance Capital of Greenwich (Connecticut) is a company that specializes in buy-side stock market introductions: http://www.renaissancecapital.com.

addition, the accuracy of all multiples (based on accounting data) decreases at the end of the first day of trading.

Earnings per share used[26]	Absolute prediction error		Regression of the percentage of valuations included at least 15% of the current P/E
	Mean	Median	
Historical accounting data at 1 year	55%	52.1%	15.4%
Forecast data for the current year	43.7%	40.1%	18.9%
Forecast data for the next fiscal year	28.5%	22.2%	36.4%

Table 2.5. *Error between current P/E multiple and forecast P/E according to the second criteria of the second standard*

Earnings per share used	Absolute prediction error		Regression of the percentage of valuations included at least 15% of the current P/E
	Mean	Median	
Forecast data for the current financial year (young companies)	31.9%	26.2%	29.2%
Forecast data for the current year (old companies)	23%	18.8%	40.8%

Table 2.6. *Error between the current P/E and forecast P/E multiples between young and old companies of the sample according to the second standard*

The more the valuations by the P/E are based on forecast data over time, the more precise they become. The forecast data for the following fiscal year has the lowest mean and median errors and more than a third of within this section provide valuations below 15% of the current value of the P/E.

By distinguishing the "young" from the "old" companies, we find that it is easier to make a better assessment of the latter over the former.

26 The selected companies all have positive EPS.

	Absolute prediction error		Regression of the percentage of valuations that are included at less than 15% of the current multiple
	Mean	Median	
	Economic value of equity/turnover		
Historical accounting data at 1 year	56%	46.3%	13.3%
Forecast data for the current year	54.6%	44%	15.4%
	Enterprise value/turnover		
Historical accounting data at 1 year	52.8%	42.6%	16.1%
Data	52.1%	41.8%	13.3%
	Enterprise value/operating cash flow		
Historical accounting data at 1 year	43.2%	37.5%	20.3%
Forecast data at the current year	41.6%	34.1%	21.7%

Table 2.7. *Error between the current value of the multiples and the predicted values of multiples according to the criteria of the second benchmark*

Turnover used	Parameter estimates		Absolute error prediction		Percentage regression of valuations within 15% of the current multiple
	Profitability multiple	Growth multiple	Mean	Median	
Historical accounting data at 1 year	0.171	/	50.3%	40.4%	18.2%
Forecast data for the current year	0.218	0.199	48.8%	40.1%	18.9%

Table 2.8. *Error between the current turnover multiple and the forecasted values of the turnover multiple that incorporates a profitability multiple and growth multiple according to the criteria of the second benchmark*

The multiple that is most precise is the one that relates enterprise value to operating cash flow. Indeed, the mean and the median are the lowest, and the regressions for the valuation percentage included within 15% of the current multiple are the highest. Furthermore, the results confirm that the forecasted values confer more accuracy. Kim and Ritter also perform tests on these multiples by separating young from old companies. They come to the same conclusions about whether the oldest companies provide the best valuations: the multiples of the oldest companies that relate enterprise value to operating cash flow are 38%, below 15% of the present value of this same multiple.

The two researchers finally adjust their turnover multiple to apply it to the aggregate of the company undergoing its IPO. By incorporating the factor of profitability in addition to the factor of growth (when it comes to forecast data), we have:

$$xT_i = \frac{EV}{T}\text{sect} + \text{ Profitability factor} \qquad [2.187]$$

$$+\text{Growth factor}$$

$$xT_i = \frac{EV}{T}\text{sect} + \frac{\frac{OCF_i}{T_i}}{\frac{OCF}{T}\text{sect}} + \{1; 0\} \qquad [2.188]$$

where:

– xT_i = multiple of turnover to be applied to company *i* which is undergoing valuation (going public);

– $\frac{EV}{T}\text{sect}$ = multiple of sectoral turnover;

– $\frac{OCF_i}{T_i}$ = ratio of operating cash flow to the turnover of company *i* to be valued (going public);

– $\frac{OCF}{T}\text{sect}$ = ratio of operating cash flow to sectoral turnover;

– 1 if $\Delta\ T_i$ between year *n* and $n – 1 > \Delta\ T_{sect}$ between year *n* and $n – 1$;

– 0 if $\Delta\ T_i$ between year *n* and $n – 1 < \Delta\ CA_{sect}$ between year *n* and $n – 1$.

The turnover multiple gives more precision. Indeed, based on forecast data for the current year, the coefficient for the profitability factor of 0.218 associated with the *t-statistic* of 4.18 suggests that a 20% premium should be offered to companies that are two times more profitable than the average. In addition, the growth factor with a coefficient of 0.199 also confirms that a premium of 20% must be considered for high-growth companies that list their capital on the stock market. Kim and Ritter's results reflect a certain practice: the premium offered generally ranges between 10 and 20%. The latter that investment bankers add to the initial offer price when using accounting information is the result of any additional information they have on market expectations.

The P/E is an appropriate method for valuating companies with similar financial structures, the benchmark of which can be optimized by setting it up alongside companies in the same industry with similar asset values. In addition, multiples provide appropriate valuations during an IPO. However, it seems particularly difficult to express a value in specific contexts such as in the presence of companies with significant intangible assets or during a situation of bankruptcy due to administrative and strategic biases punctuating the procedure.

Lie and Lie (2002) find in their study that companies with activities that relate to advanced technology or with significant research and development activities can be particularly difficult to evaluate. Indeed, a large proportion of their value lies in future growth opportunities. In addition, the high degree of expenditure on research and development reduces the operating result, even though the latter can be synonymous as future investments. Thus, when relying on the multiples method which is based on income statement aggregates, the estimate is likely to be skewed. For example, by isolating the 27 "dot-com" companies from their sample, Lie and Lie find that no valuation is less than 15% of the market value of the companies in question, according to the turnover multiple and the assets multiple. They note that only two of them have positive results. The results are scarcely more precise when they apply the multiples method to pharmaceutical companies and groups where research and development expenses exceed 10% of the book value of the assets. They note, however, that the most precise multiple is that of operating profit, unlike more general cases. Therefore, the multiples method is limited when it comes to valuing companies with growth potential and holding intangible assets in large quantity.

Valuation has a central place in the negotiations of bankrupt companies. Indeed, the estimated value of the business in this situation determines the value of the assets to be distributed among the different parties to allow payments and collections. However, bankruptcy is an administrative process and the factors that lead to a reliable estimate of value in a normal market process are absent. In addition, it is difficult for analysts to rely on past bankruptcy situations as they are still too rare to be able to make predictions after the fact. The valuation is therefore more complex and less precise.

According to Damodaran (2009), a young company is characterized by the absence of historical results, a phase of growth that is still to be initiated, low turnover, significant losses linked to operations, dependence on private capital that entails power dynamics, few liquid investments and a very low survival rate. According to Watson and Everett's study (1996) of nearly 5,200 Australian start-ups, 64% of them fail within 10 years, the annual bankruptcy rate being 9%. Thus, the very characteristics of young companies lead us to consider problems inherent in the process of valuation.

2.3.3. *Two delicate contexts for valuation: the bankruptcy situation and the start-up company*

American legislation regarding the administration of bankrupt companies, through Chapter 11, regulates bankruptcy circumstances by promoting the continuity of the company. The objective is to save jobs and preserve the economic system, while leaving room to maneuver for a company restructure. Chapter 11, however, emphasizes negotiation. The reorganization plan is based on an estimate of the value of the company to be restructured. The management of the bankrupt company retains control throughout the process, with an exclusive right to initiate the reorganization plan. Disagreeable creditors can vote against the plan or collect more complainants to influence the vote. They can also lobby for an alternative value to be considered, form an official committee or link up with management to develop a better plan that serves their interests. In some cases, when the plan is based on a valuation that is low enough to empower senior debt holders, the latter gain the so-called support of management by offering them jobs, stocks and/or options in the reorganized company. Creditors can ask the court to withdraw management exclusivity from the management of the bankrupt company and file a concurrent reorganization plan. Alternatively, they can request a formal valuation hearing. The most common reason for requesting an assessment hearing is to estimate whether the reorganization plan is "fair and equitable"[27]. In practice, appraisal hearings and competing plans are relatively rare for large public companies

27 Section 1129(b)(2) of the American Bankruptcy Code.

that find themselves in bankruptcy. In general, cash flow forecasts and the values they imply derive from legal actions that relate to diverging economic interests.

Hotchkiss and Mooradian (1998) examine the characteristics of 55 transactions of bankrupt companies that were taken over by listed companies and reconcile their results with 55 other transactions carried out between healthy companies. They find that 66% of bankruptcy takeovers are carried out by companies that have at least one type of activity in common[28]. By way of comparison, Kaplan and Weisbach (1992) carry out a similar study around acquisitions of companies that do not find themselves in a situation of bankruptcy, and their results indicate that the offeror and the target (with at least one type of activity in common) represent only 33% of transactions. To measure the correlation between an acquisition, Hotchkiss and Mooradian follow the methodology used by Kaplan and Weisbach based on the American classification of SIC according to the Standard and Poor's register. That is to say, an acquisition is linked to three levels of figures if one of the four activities, which is the most important to the acquirer and the target (classified according to turnover), correspond to this same level of code. To complete their analysis, Hotchkiss and Mooradian note that, for a healthy number of transactions, the target and the acquirer have previously entered into a relationship. This is the case when, for example, the offeror already owns the assets of the target.

As a result, and knowing that the target and the acquirer operate in related activities, there is an information asymmetry problem in the market, which has the consequence of dissuading potential offers from less well-informed companies. This therefore justifies that targets in default are often bought by companies in the same industry. However, this does not prevent there from being more competitive bidding than for transactions between companies that are not in a situation of bankruptcy. In their sample, 18 of the 55 buyout transactions (32.7%) of bankrupt companies had multiple offers from potential buyers, while only 11 of the 55 transactions (20%) between "healthy" companies came across such a multitude of propositions.

The work of Bradley *et al.* (1988) and Bange and Mazzeo (1997) also supports this observation. Indeed, the former find multiple offers for 73 of

---

28 Two companies have the same activity when the first four digits of their classification, according to SIC, are the same.

the 236 transactions studied (or 31%), and the latter find multiple offers for 103 of the 436 transactions studied (or 23.6%). In addition, the relative size of targets in the situation of bankruptcy is on average 25.8% of that of the acquirer, based on total assets and 30.2% based on total sales. The conclusions of Clark and Ofek (1994) that also concern the study of a sample of mergers are equivalent.

	Mean	Median
Turnover multiple		
EV of the target company in the situation of bankruptcy/ turnover	1.1	0.4
Median EV of a sector of activity/turnover	1.6	1.1
EV of transactions between "healthy" companies/turnover	2.3	1.1
Asset multiple		
EV of the target company in the situation of bankruptcy/VcA	0.7	0.5
Median EV of the sector of activity/VcA	1.3	1.2
EV of transactions between "healthy" companies/VcA	1.9	1.2
Price paid in relation to the value that comes from the benchmarks		
Price paid/turnover multiple of the sector of activity	45.1%	60.5%
Price paid/turnover multiple of transactions between "healthy" companies	43.5%	68.8%
Price paid/asset multiple of the sector of activity	45.7%	64.7%
Price paid/asset multiple of transactions between "healthy" companies	40.2%	59.6%

Table 2.9. *Characteristics of bankruptcy buyout transactions compared to two benchmarks (EV: enterprise value; turnover; VcA: book value of assets)*

The multiples of target companies in bankruptcy are lower than the other two benchmarks, and the asset multiple is lower, which even leads us to undervalue a company that finds itself in this situation. The prices paid (which are calculated on the basis of the turnover multiple or assets multiple) to buy out bankrupt companies are, on average, 45% lower than the corresponding transactions between healthy companies in the same sector of activity. In other words, even though the prices paid are generally lower compared to the two benchmarks considered, the asymmetry of the information that resides in the market will dissuade companies that do not belong to the same industry.

Gilson *et al.* (2000) compare the market value of the shares of 63 public enterprises restructured after a situation of bankruptcy with their estimates from projections of their cash flows and their reorganization plans[29]. To the extent that practitioners suggest that the first share prices after the restructuring plan may experience downward trends as the company's creditors seek to sell the shares they received under the terms of the restructuring plan, the three researchers examine valuation errors based on the discounted market value of equity at 1 month, 3 months and 6 months after the date of the first listing of the share, following the restructuring plan. The distribution mechanism of shares under a restructuring plan is not the same for the whole sample of companies. Eberhart *et al.* (1998) convey in their work the problems posed by determining the post-bankruptcy stock price. In this way, it so happens that the pre-bankruptcy share is canceled and a new issue takes place or the old share remains and an issue is added. Valuations are based on the DCF method and the comparables method. Indeed, according to the work of Scarberry *et al.* (1996), these methods are widely used in practice. Regarding their method of discounting cash flows, Gilson, Hotchkiss and Ruback do not depend on using free cash flows but rather on capital cash flows (CCF). The difference between the two methods is that CCFs measure the money available to all holders (and lenders) of capital and include tax savings on financial interest and other tax benefits. In addition, the CCF method values the company by discounting the CCF at the cost of capital that corresponds to a set of companies that present the same industrial risk. Like the classic DCF method, the CCF approach incorporates a terminal value to represent the present value of the cash flows after the projection period.

However, in the previously analyzed article of his, Ruback (1998) demonstrates algebraically that the two approaches are equivalent[30]. Therefore, the three researchers decide to rely on the CCF method, since the capital structures of the companies in their sample generally change during the forecast period, and therefore it is easier to consider a single rate of discounting rather than recalculating the weighted average cost of capital

29 The three researchers explain that the quality of the data in the sample varies. Some companies provide clear explanations as to the assumptions that are applied to their projections when, for others, it has been necessary to resort to the assumptions made by the authors themselves in terms of tax rates, working capital requirements or capital expenditure. About half of the companies had made projects of 5 to 10 years, almost a fifth of less than 4 years.

30 This method is developed in section 2.2.1.

that is essential for discounting free cash flows at each period. In addition, the CCF approach is more appropriate given the complicated tax situations of the companies contained within the sample. It updates all cash flows by including forecast tax shields at the cost of assets pre-tax, unlike the APV method, which discounts the tax shield at the cost of debt. Thus, the CCF method assumes that the level of debt is maintained such that the tax benefits do not modify the level of risk of the company. Gilson (1997) shows that debt ratios generally do not change after a few years after the event of bankruptcy. Akin to the DCF method, once the projection period ends, the forecast should be extended. The terminal value is determined using a constant growth rate, which is assumed to be infinite. However, a distinction needs to be made between the two stages, as these bankrupt companies have incurred losses and, as a result, they have tax deferrals that must first be taken into account. Regarding the appraisal by comparables, Gilson *et al.* rely on the gross operating surplus multiple.

	Valuation using the CCF method	**Valuation using the EBITDA multiple method**
Median	-0.6%	4.7%
Mean	-9.1%	-10.4%
Standard deviation	54.6%	79.4%
Percentage under 15% error	25.4%	21%
Maximum	95.2%	115.8%
Minimum	-173.5%	-269.3%

Table 2.10. *Comparing evaluation errors*[31] *on the basis of the CCF method and the EBITDA multiple method*

Even though the medians for the percentage of valuation errors seem slim (particularly for the CCF method), the work of the three researchers nevertheless leads to dispersions of such magnitude that we can characterize the valuations as imprecise. The ratio of the sample of estimated value to market value varies from less than 270% to more than 115% for the comparables method by the multiple of EBITDA, and from less than 173% to more than 95% for the CCF method. We thus can come to the same type of conclusions as Kaplan and Ruback (1995) for a sample of companies that

31 Valuation errors are calculated from the logarithmic ratio between the estimates value and the market value of the business.

benefit from the leverage effect with regard to how imprecise the traditional valuation methods are in specific situations where cash flows are difficult to predict due to structural changes. However, Gilson *et al.* do not attribute the disparity of error between forecasts and the reality of values solely to choosing the wrong models or due to their assumptions being weak when it comes to the discount rate or the forecasted long-term growth rate, nor even to the fact that the values of the post-bankruptcy stock price cannot be representative if we consider the work of Eberhart *et al.* mentioned above. Indeed, according to the statistical tests carried out by the three researchers, the medians of evaluation error remain close to zero, and the differences in the means of absolute error (about 38% for the CCF method and 46% for the EBITDA multiple) are negligible, whether we are looking at the day of the first listing, or 1 month, 3 months or 6 months after the restructuring. It is therefore possible to express the inaccuracy of these valuations, by stating that the administrative process which is initiated during bankruptcy limits the quality of the information available, thus compromising the market process. As proof of this, they find that errors are less significant when the company's stock has remained listed throughout the entire reorganization phase. Thus, potential buyers in the market have less incentive to glean information from the bankrupt company whose stock is temporarily withdrawn from the market. The three researchers then set out to show that valuations are made more accurate when they rely on forecasts from financial analysts – insofar as they are available (about 20% of the sample) – and not those from management. We can thus see that the error percentage below 15% goes from 25.4 to 30.8% based on the CCF method using only financial analyst forecasts and from 21 to 46.2% based on the EBITDA multiple method using financial analyst forecasts only.

Drawing on previous work by Gilson (1995), the three researchers uncover a second explanation to justify the discrepancies between their estimates and the situation in reality. Strategic biases according to the actors involved have important consequences in terms of value. An underestimated value benefits the parties (creditors, management) who receive shares (and/or stock options) once the restructuring has finished. Thus, creditors that hold senior debts see their claims grow and gain momentum. It is therefore in their interest for cash flows to be underestimated. Junior debt holders take the opposite view: overestimating the value of the stock increases the likelihood that they will collect debt. The strategic biases that justify valuation errors can be explained through the bargaining power balance between the various stakeholders, the shares held by members of the management in place and the existence of external offers to acquire or invest in the company in bankruptcy and change of management. Gilson *et al.* perform regression tests on valuation errors and show that the estimated values tend to be lower when the creditor takes control of the reorganized company, by exchanging a large part of its senior debt, but the estimated values tend to be higher when creditors use junior debt to gain control. Estimated values are also smaller when management receives stock or options after the restructuring plan, which turns out to be a blessing to management. Finally, the estimated values are lower when the companies issue new shares and a third-party investor subscribes to them after the restructuring plan. The three researchers suggest that valuations are strategically used in a trade process in order to promote the desired trade-off. In other words, the economic interests of different parties impact the forecast of cash flows used.

According to Damodaran (2009), the valuation of a start-up through the DCF method creates difficulties when forecasting cash flows from existing assets. However, for some start-ups, the assets represent such a small share of value that extending the analysis to the future resources provided would not cover the full-value potential. The valuation of other companies (for whom existing assets might allow the value to become more precise) is hampered by the scarcity of available information or by its inability to effectively forecast the future. The lack of historical data and the preponderance of expenses that can be three or four times greater than the current turnover will deteriorate the quality of the calculation. In addition, it is difficult to distinguish the expenses that are related to more or less distant future benefits from more traditional operating expenses. Moreover, the growth rate that is to be applied – which is a consequence of the quality of new investments and the profitability of existing assets – is difficult to estimate if we consider a few elements. These are if turnover is absent or has been irregular in the past, if losses are carried over that destroy our ability to anticipate and evolve margins, and profitability rates which neglect the impossibility of considering "the quality of growth", i.e. the amount that the company will reinvest on the assumption that the profitability of capital is higher than its cost. Valuation by the DCF method also requires us to determine a discount rate. Usually, a company's risk assessment depends on the price of the securities that are issued. Thus, we estimate the equity beta by performing a regression on the returns of a stock with those of the linked market index; the cost of debt is determined based on the current bond price. Additionally, traditional risk and return models that are used to estimate the cost of capital own funds focus only on market risk, i.e. risk that cannot be diversified on the assumption that investors have diversified their risk themselves.

Studying start-ups challenges this method of analysis. Most of them have neither their capital nor bonds listed. Thus, it is difficult to run regressions without historical returns to obtain a beta or use a market interest rate on the debt. To complicate this further, the capital of young companies is often held by investors who have either fully invested in the company as founders or by investors who have only partially diversified their risk (venture capital funds). Therefore, the above assumption of asserting that the risk is diversified cannot be considered. Finally, the capital of a start-up can come from multiple sources over time. This can therefore lead us to consider different equity costs and different types of shares that are unlike a public issue. Terminal value is a large part of the total value of a traditional business. For a young company, this seems to be all the more pertinent. Therefore, it is a question of determining the assumptions about when the young company will achieve stable growth (if it achieves it in view of the high rate of bankruptcy it has to endure) and the characteristics that are related to the level of stability that is found.

Damodaran then evokes the difficulties attached to evaluating certain multiples. In light of the large loss carry-overs, it does not appear that the P/E and EBITDA multiples are suitable. The "book value" multiple does not reflect the real capital that is invested in the company, given the low figure that it would indicate is linked to the recent existence of the company. In addition, it is difficult to try to make comparisons with even public companies that belong to the same industry given their differences in risk, cash flow generated and growth potential. Also, comparison with other young companies can be compromised: they are too rarely listed. Moreover, it is difficult to determine the best risk indicator. The beta or standard deviation of stock returns (volatility) is often used as a measure of equity risk. However, the information needed to calculate these measures is not available for young private companies whose existence is still too recent. The risk of bankruptcy also remains a problem. The relative value of a business increases when its probability of survival increases, and putting this process into practice is no easy task. Finally, a problem arises as to the adjustments of the different forms of shares and their ability to be liquidated. Damodaran develops the method used by some analysts to valuate a young company. Without considering the details that are attached to cash flow, the assessment should focus on sales or bottom line. In addition, they recommend focusing on the short term: 2–5 years of business plans, which must coincide with the forecast for the resale of the business via venture capital funds. Equity value at the end of the forecasted period can be obtained by applying the sector's P/E to net income. The enterprise value at the end of the period can be obtained by applying the revenue multiple of the sector to that of the enterprise expected at the end of the forecasted period. Then, to obtain a present value, the estimated value at the end of the forecasted period must be discounted to a target rate of return, set high enough relative to the discount rates applied to listed companies to capture both the perception of risk and the likelihood that the business will not survive[32]:

$$V_E = \frac{V_{En}}{(1+r)^n} \qquad [2.189]$$

where:

– V_E: current equity value;

– V_{En}: equity value at the end of forecast period n;

– r: target rate of return.

Finally, in order to obtain the share ownership in capital P, we calculate the ratio between the injection of funds made by the shareholder in question I and the sum of the enterprise value obtained, thanks to the multiple of turnover EV and the injection of funds I. In other words, we have:

$$P = \frac{I}{\frac{EV}{T}+I} \qquad [2.190]$$

In comparison to internal transactions, public offerings engage companies in large and rapid growth and business restructuring projects. Theoretically, acquisitions can be a source of value creation through the operational synergies that are generated, resulting from the implementation of economies of scale, financial synergies linked to the increase in debt capacity and the disciplinary effects of a takeover of the team that leads the target company. However, empirical studies of these mergers conclude that the acquisitions do not create or create little value for the initiating

32 According to Damodaran's research, the typical target rate of return for a start-up is between 50% and 70%, while the target rate for an IPO is between 25% and 30%.

companies. According to Bessière (2008), the motivations of buyers for this type of transaction are, in fact, linked to strategic interests, i.e. to a desire to extend their "empire" or, in accordance with agency theory, to a quest for power on the part of the directors to the detriment of the interests of the shareholders.

2.4. The creation of value resulting from control operations

Hotchkiss and Mooradian (1998) study the creation of value from the buyout transactions of failing firms. They find that in the days that follow the transaction, stock prices rise for both the bankrupt target and the company that is initiating the buyout. However, this type of action between healthy companies causes a price increase only for the target. Thus, the takeover of a bankrupt company can be an effective way to redeploy assets. The more comprehensive study by Moeller *et al.* (2004) found that after a takeover, there is, on average, decreased value. These conclusions raise questions about the value of carrying out this type of transaction, at least between healthy companies. It results that executives may wish to acquire new targets relating to reasons of power and to compensation opportunities. Second, errors of judgment through too much optimism are able to justify these actions. Indeed, managers can overestimate the expected value creation after buyout operations.

2.4.1. *The creation of value from the buyout of companies in bankruptcy*

In order to determine whether the takeover of bankrupt firms generates economic gains, Hotchkiss and Mooradian (1998) examine and compare the performance of cash flow after the merger, based on the results found by Hotchkiss (1995) from a previous study, to that of the transactions between healthy companies. They thus observe an improvement in the cash flow that results from the merger between the supplier and the company in a situation of bankruptcy, relative to about 5% in year N + 1 after the transaction, and 6% in year N + 2, whereas the sample corresponding to 55 business acquisitions without a default situation does not reveal any significant change. The increase in profitability for the first group of companies results from a reduction in operating and employment costs. By focusing on the notion of value creation, the two researchers note, moreover, that the market perceives this type of acquisition favorably. Stock prices increase for both the target in bankruptcy and the acquirer in the days that follow the announcement of the transaction. Transactions between healthy companies cause a price increase only for the target and not for the supplier. This market reaction is explained by the fact that company executives find that acquiring a company in bankruptcy is less attractive, as it requires resorting to complex negotiations with creditors and courts. Thus, it seems reasonable to consider that there are less "bad acquirers" for a sample of acquisitions of bankrupt companies. Taking over a company in such a situation connotes prospects and a real desire for growth in the market. Therefore, the buyout of companies in bankruptcy can facilitate the redeployment of assets to improve their efficiency. This correlates to the assumption according to which companies that operate in the same industry as the target have better information and/or expertise when it comes to the level of efficiency when redeploying the assets of the bankrupt company. Additionally, despite the fact that many bankrupt business buyers are heavily indebted and operate in a struggling industry, acquisitions on average lead to improved operational performance.

2.4.2. *Abnormal returns resulting from control operations*

The work of Moeller *et al.* (2004) leads us to consider that value is destroyed after the control operations have been completed. By building a sample of 4,136 American transactions, they study, between 1998 and 2001, the evolution of the market capitalizations of the buyers 1 day before and 1 day after the announcement of the transaction, and note a loss of about $240 billion. This reduction comes to $220 billion when they extend the testing period from 1980 to 2001, which refers to 12,023 transactions. Then, Moeller *et al.* (2005) are interested in how profitable acquisitions are. If traditionally the profitability of buyers around the announcement date is significantly lower than the recorded profitability of the targets, it is necessary to qualify this result. Indeed, insofar as the size of the targets is most often less than that of the acquirers, the expected gain represents a higher proportion of the value of the target, which logically leads to higher returns for the targets. Considering a combined approach helps to better understand the operation. This is carried out by portfolio (between buyers or between targets in particular) and more specifically by pairing target and acquirers within the same transaction. The latter method allows for a precise measurement of value creation per transaction and its distribution between both companies. The two-way approach, used by Moeller *et al.*, is based on studying events. It consists of comparing the profitability of the share observed during the announcement with a theoretical profitability that is considered normal and determined using the CAPM. This results in a so-called abnormal profitability, which makes it possible to measure the effect of the transaction for the shareholders. This abnormal profitability is calculated and accumulated over a time window (from less than 1 day before the announcement to more than 1 day after the announcement in this case). This measure assumes that the effects of the acquisition are incorporated into the prices as soon as the transaction is announced and that the normal returns estimation model correctly predicts the returns that would have been observed in the absence of events. The study by the three researchers confirms that acquisitions create little value (1.35% between 1980 and 2001) and that buyers also receive little (1.1% over the same period).

Periods	Number of operations	Cumulative abnormal returns [J - 1, J + 1]	
		Acquirers	Acquirers and targets[33]
1980–1990	2,182	0.0064	0.0241
1991–2001	9,841	0.0120	0.0104
1998–2001	4,136	0.0069	0.0029
1980–2001	12,023	0.0110	0.0135

Table 2.11. *Low profitability of acquisitions according to Moeller et al. (2005)*

The factors that determine abnormal returns depend on the characteristics of the supply, the companies themselves and their strategic objectives. As a result, abnormal returns for buyers are lower when the offer is hostile, has been the subject of upbids or is carried out via a public offering to exchange rather than a public offering to buy. In addition, abnormal returns are lower when the acquirer is of a significant size, with little debt, possibly with significant cash flow, low proportions of shareholder–manager and with anti-takeover measures. Finally, abnormal returns are lower when the acquisition results from a conglomerate operation as opposed to operations that are focused on the same business sector. In this context, Pécherot (2000) introduces a ternary measure diversification that is no longer binary. Using a

33 Portfolio of buyers and targets (with profitability being weighted by market capitalization).

sample of 80 French acquisitions over the 1977–1993 period, he distinguishes between dominant mergers where the main activity is the same between target and acquirer, and linked mergers where the main activity of the target is identical to one of the secondary activities of the acquirer, and unrelated mergers where the activity of the target is not present at all for the acquirer. By studying the abnormal long-term returns from a two-factor model (beta and size), he concludes that unrelated diversification is a source of value destruction (-19.82%); a dominant merger has no significant effect and that only related diversification creates value (+ 27.21% over 3 years).

Consequently, the empirical work presented shows that takeover operations converge towards a destruction of value or, in the best case, towards a weak creation of value for the shareholders of the initiating company. This then raises questions as to the motivations of managers to lead their companies into such operations.

2.4.3. *The motivation of buyers to initiate control operations*

Executives do not necessarily aim to make decisions that maximize shareholder wealth. Their actions may be more oriented towards opportunistic policies in order to develop the size of the group. In this case, their motivations are linked to the search for power and the increase in their remuneration in particular. These constitute governance mechanisms. Empirical studies therefore question the possible link between the profitability of buyers and their mode of governance. In the case of acquisitions, the results generally admit effective governance. Amihud *et al.* (1990) show that the abnormal returns of buyers are lower, or even negative, when managers hold less than 5% of the capital. Lewellen *et al.* (1985) reveal a positive relationship between the abnormal returns of buyers and the share of capital held by managers. However, there are multiple governance mechanisms that relate to the concentration of shareholders, the composition of the board of directors, the composition of the directors' share in capital, their method of remuneration (indexed to the share price) and debt level. These interacting mechanisms are the subject of studies dispersed to the extent that their degree of efficiency and characteristics differ from company to company. Masulis *et al.* (2007) attempt to overcome this problem by looking at the consequences of governance. They are based on a governance index that is based on the absence of anti-takeover measures[34]. Thus, a company that has anti-takeover protection will see its manager being put under less pressure, which means they are more likely to commit to undertake unprofitable projects. The researchers test this hypothesis using the abnormal returns observed during the announcement of 3,333 acquisitions over the period 1990–2003 in the United States. They construct two governance indices: one from 24 anti-takeover measures from the initiator and the other from six measures. Then, they establish two portfolios for each index: the first is called "democrat", i.e. good governance, and the other is called "dictator", i.e. weak governance. They therefore observe positive cumulative abnormal returns (CAR) over the time window [J - 2; J + 2] of the date of the transaction, which is only for buyers with strong governance and significantly higher than that for buyers with weak governance.

CAR in %	"Democrat" portfolio (1)	"Dictator" portfolio (2)	(1) – (2)
Classification according to 24 anti-takeover criteria			
Mean	0.468	- 0.050	0.518
Median	0.386	- 0.220	0.606
Number of observations	1,708	1,625	–
Classification according to 6 anti-takeover criteria			
Mean	0.572	- 0.241	0.813
Median	0.435	- 0.303	0.738
Number of observations	1,872	1,461	–

Table 2.12. *Difference in profitability for buyers with strong and weak governance during the announcement of an acquisition according to Masuslis et al. (2007)*

While managerial opportunism may explain low returns among buyers, we should not overlook the possibility that managers may make errors of judgment when evaluating the target. Out of overconfidence and optimism, they may overestimate the value creation expected after the transaction.

34 These measures are supposed to be present in companies where the manager is uncontrolled when seeking to consolidate their position and to exempt themselves from governance by the market.

Thus, the behavior of a manager who is not perfectly rational can lead them to anticipate excessive future cash flows and to misunderstand the extent of the risk. Roll (1986) assumes that acquisitions are made because managers anticipate value creation. However, *hubris*[35] encourages them to overestimate this value creation. Consequently, empirical studies about acquisitions are biased when they justify the negative returns observed. However, it seems tricky to assess and test the level of hubris. Hambrick and Hiller (2005) construct a hubris index using three variables: the description of the leader in the press, the 1-year performance of the stock market price (strong confidence that promotes excessive confidence and optimism) and the compensation of the leader compared to that of the second highest paid leader in the company (reflecting the relative level of self-esteem). They find that there is a strong correlation between these three variables and bid premiums.

2.5. Conclusion

Taking into account taxation of capital gains, dividends and interest received and with regard to risk aversion, investors calculate the potential benefit of their personal leverage. As a result, the financial policy of the company is impacted. In addition, information asymmetry and the concurrent agency conflicts, which emerge, in particular, during mergers and acquisitions and which are more significant when the target company is in bankruptcy also influence the choice regarding the company's financial structure. The latter thus turns out to be more optimized than optimal, given the divergence in interests held by the various stakeholders. The exercise of valuing the company in a reliable and relevant manner remains, therefore, a delicate task. Beyond the quality of the assumptions to be determined when it comes to the business plan or forecasted aggregates and the ease of putting a model into practice, the choice of an approach to determine a "fair" value depends on the context in which the company finds itself. Indeed, the valuation of repurchases from a financial arrangement with leverage seems to be more adequate using a method of discounting cash flows. On the other hand, if the analyst was able to constitute, at the very least, a homogeneous benchmark in terms of business sector, financial structure and asset value, the P/E appears to be an effective solution for estimating the value of a target company. In absolute terms, the asset multiple provides better estimates.

35 Hubris means excessive self-confidence.

When looking at a start-up company, considering the turnover, the bottom line and the target return as part of a short-term business plan seem to be the most appropriate criteria that mean this estimation exercise is effectively carried out. In the event of a target's bankruptcy situation, even though the revenue multiple and the asset multiple are ratios used to value a company, the prices paid depend more on the negotiating power between the different stakeholders. Moreover, following the operations carried out to buy out a bankrupted company, the stock market prices go up for both the target company and the acquiring company in the days that follow the transaction. This increase in stock price mechanism only comes to the fore for the target company during a buyout operation between healthy companies. The reason for this is that the market assumes that only good buyers engage in the buyout of companies at risk, given the administrative constraints that this process creates. Thus, we will anticipate the implementation of a real growth plan. More generally, repurchase operations lead to the destruction of value. However, insider executives may be able to perceive in these operations, should they continue to occur, the possibility of being able to influence the market and increase their compensation.

Conclusion

The exercise of valuing a company and the equity of its shareholders is prominent and complex for each of the company's interlocutors, especially when it comes to intervening in the control market, both when it comes to purchase and to sale. It is permanent because it is the basis of all negotiations, all offers and all transactions that make building the strategy to be adopted possible. It is complex because it is based on three traditional methods, which, as Ruback (1998) uncovered, can be adjusted. In addition, depending on particular contexts, they can be variably reliable and relevant, depending, in particular, on the quality of the assumptions, projections and benchmarks.

In a balanced market, valuation methods should lead to the same result. However, in practice, there will always be differences. Traditional valuation methods are therefore relevant and reliable due to the strategic direction given by the values that are found and due to their level of usefulness when applied to particular contexts in the company's life cycle.

If the asset value is greater than the proprietary approach and the DCF method (Le Fur 2010), the company is worth more through its past (revalued equity) than through its future prospects for profitability. It is advisable to divest by liquidating the assets in order to obtain a better level of profitability and a more effective allocation of resources. This type of process, which proved to be very popular in the 1980s and 2007–2008[1], consisted of buying listed companies (take-over bid) and selling them in parts. The buyer will then yield a capital gain, the sum of the parts being

1 Breakup of ABN-Amro, Scottish and New Castle, Hagemayer, etc.

greater than the value of the entire business. If the asset value is lower than the other two methods (the most frequent case in an economy being characterized by the importance of intangible assets (Ernst and Young 2007)), the company is highly profitable, enabling investment in projects with a level of profitability that is higher than the cost of capital, which is equal to a certain level of know-how and strategic positioning (barriers to entry). The starting point for mixing methods is to determine economic assets that are corrected for any capital gain or loss. A normative operating result can be calculated by applying a required rate of return on the economic asset. The difference between the operating profit anticipated in the business plan and the normative results will either show a “super profit” (goodwill) or a deficit. Conceptually, this “super profit” corresponds to an annuity that the purchaser is prepared to purchase. Goodwill can be used over a shorter or longer period of time, in order to correct asset values by considering the anticipated economic profitability and by valuing intangible capital. These can then be updated. If the value obtained via the multiples method is greater than that obtained from the DCF, it may be wise to go public because investors are able to appreciate the risk and profitability of the company more than the current shareholder. Conversely, if the value that results from the multiples is lower, it is preferable to wait for the company to realize its growth potential, which is reflected according to the projections that come from the DCF method.

In theory, there is no reason why a buyer or seller will favor one valuation method over another. But, in practice (Vernimmen 2012), a seller will typically prefer the DCF method because its foundation resides in a questionably optimistic business plan. The comparables method can be considered because it will be difficult to agree to sell securities at a lower price than a competitor, and an IPO can represent an alternative to sale. A buyer will base their negotiation on the comparables method, in order to justify a lower price than that which comes from the DCF method (Bonnet-Bernard 2008). However, the buyer may consider the DCF approach because it is specified on their post-acquisition plan of actions (synergies, developments, etc.) upon which the future profitability of the acquisition depends. Therefore, the value that comes from the DCF method, applied to a business plan that is deemed realistic, effectively corresponds to the price that can be agreed to without destroying value for shareholders (Bouchikhi 2008).

Depending on specific contexts, financial literature advocates the use of certain methods to the detriment of others. In leveraged buyout transactions, Kaplan and Ruback (1995) recommend the use of methods based on discounting cash flows from business plans. Lie and Lie (2002) note that overall the asset multiple provides more effective estimates compared to other types of multiples. Alford (1992) insists on the need to use the P/E multiple in the case of homogeneous sector benchmarks in terms of financial structure and the value of economic assets. For companies in bankruptcy, Hotchkiss and Mooradian (1998) find that the prices paid are based on the turnover multiple and asset multiple. However, when it comes to start-ups, Damodaran (2009) believes that a method that relates to turnover and bottom line for which a target rate of return is applied is more appropriate.

Beyond their potential for theoretical perfectibility, which is mentioned in the financial literature by Rubacl (1998) and Arnold and North (2008) in particular, traditional valuation methods can still be subject to certain limits. Indeed, valuing a company can mean:

– strongly speculating on the future of the company and on market conditions;

– implicitly carrying out very long-term forecasts based on extrapolating past results or results in the near future, which may lead to excesses;

– sometimes forgetting that asset values are false protections.

In addition, the choice of an expected flow scenario and the irreversible nature of the investment decision do not allow us the possibility of extending if development prospects are offered. The strategic aspect then comes into play alongside purely financial techniques. Managerial flexibility is an implicit yet entirely essential characteristic. Under these conditions, approaching the process through real options can be a method that is complementary, especially in situations where there is a great level of uncertainty and when dealing with sequential development projects.

Appendix

Demonstrating the Terminal Value (TV) of DCFs

The value of operational assets V equal to the sum of the discounted future FCF is written as such:

$$V = \sum_{t=1}^{+\infty} \frac{FCF_t}{(1+K)^t} \qquad [A.1]$$

The business plan of the company to be valued only provides forecasts on *n* years.

We then split the formula into two elements:

$$V = \sum_{t=1}^{n} \frac{FCF_t}{(1+K)^t} + \sum_{t=n+1}^{+\infty} \frac{FCF_t}{(1+K)^t} \qquad [A.2]$$

We call the terminal value (TV) the sum:

$$\sum_{t=n+1}^{+\infty} \frac{FCF_t}{(1+K)^t} = \frac{FCF_{n+1}}{(1+K)^{n+1}} + \frac{FCF_{n+2}}{(1+K)^{n+2}} + \cdots \qquad [A.3]$$

To calculate it, let us suppose that the FCFs, over *n* years, at an annual growth rate of *g*:

$$\begin{aligned} TV &= \frac{(1+g)FCF_n}{(1+K)^{n+1}} + \frac{(1+g)^2 FCF_n}{(1+K)^{n+2}} + \cdots \\ &= \frac{FCF_n}{(1+K)^n}\left[\frac{(1+g)}{(1+K)} + \frac{(1+g)^2}{(1+K)^2} + \cdots\right] \end{aligned} \quad [A.4]$$

$$TV = \frac{FCF_n}{(1+K)^n}\sum_{t=1}^{+\infty}\left(\frac{1+g}{1+K}\right)^t \quad [A.5]$$

$$TV = \frac{FCF_n}{(1+K)^n}\frac{\frac{1+g}{1+K}}{1-\frac{1+g}{1+K}} = \frac{FCF_n}{(1+K)^n}\frac{\frac{1+g}{1+K}}{\frac{1+K-1-g}{1+K}} \quad [A.6]^1$$

$$TV = \frac{FCF_n}{(1+K)^n}\frac{(1+g)}{(K-g)} \quad [A.7]$$

$$V = \sum_{t=1}^{n}\frac{FCF_t}{(1+K)^t} + \frac{FCF_n}{(1+K)^n}\frac{(1+g)}{(K-g)} \quad [A.8]$$

---

1 $\sum_{t=1}^{\infty} q^t = \frac{q}{(1-q)}$ if $0 < q < 1$ so that the geometric series converges.

References

Alford, A. (1992). The effect of the set of comparable firms on the accuracy of the price-earnings valuation method. *Journal of Accounting Research*, 30(1), 94–108, Spring.

Almeida, H. and Philippon, T. (2007). The risk-adjusted cost of financial distress. *Journal of Finance*, 62, 2557–2586.

Amihud, Y., Lev, B., and Travlos, N.G. (1990). Corporate control and the choice of investment financing: The case of corporate acquisitions. *Journal of Finance*, 45, 603–616.

Amir, E. and Lev, B. (1996). Value-relevance of nonfinancial information: The case of wireless communication. *Journal of Accounting and Economics*, 22(1–3), 3–30.

Arnold, T. and North, D.S. (2008). Duration measures for corporate project valuation. *The Engineering Economist*, 53(2), 103–117.

Asker, J., Farre-Mensa, J., and Ljungqvist, A. (2011). Does the stock market harm investment incentives? Working document, ECGI Finance, Brussels.

Bae, K.H. (2011). Employee treatment and firm leverage: A test of the stakeholder theory of capital structure. *Journal of Financial Economics*, 100(1), 130–153.

Bange, M. and Mazzeo, M. (1997). When do bidders buy-pass target management? Working document, Michigan State University, Michigan.

Beaver, W. and Morse, D. (1978). What determines price-earnings ratios? *Financial Analysts Journal*, 34(4), 65–78.

Bellalah, M. (1998). *Finance moderne d'entreprise*, 1st edition, Economica, Paris.

Bessière, V. (2008). Création de valeur et motivations des acquisitions d'entreprises. *Banque & marchés*, 94, May–June.

Blazenko, G. (1987). Managerial preference, asymmetric information and financial structure. *Journal of Finance*, 42, 839–862.

Boatsman, J.R. and Baskin, E.F. (1981). Asset valuation with incomplete markets. *The Accounting Review*, 56(1), 38–53.

Bodie, Z., Kane, A., and Marcus, A.J. (2004). *Investments*, 6th edition, McGraw-Hill, New York.

Bonnet-Bernard, S. (2008). Primes et décotes dans le cadre des évaluations financières. Report, SFEV, Paris.

Bouchikhi, H. (2008). Le business plan est aussi un vecteur d'apprentissage. *Les échos*, June, 10–11.

Bradley, M., Desai, A., and Kim, E. (1988). Synergistic gains from corporate acquisitions and their division between the stockholders of targets and acquiring firms. *Journal of Financial Economics*, 21(1), 3–40.

Brealey, R., Myers, S., and Allen, F. (2007). *Principes de gestion financière*, 8th edition, Pearson Education, London.

Brennan, M.J. (1970). Taxes, market valuation and corporate financial policy. *National Tax Journal*, 23(4), 417–427.

Charreaux, G. (1997). *Le gouvernement des entreprises, corporate governance, théorie et faits*. Economica, Paris.

Chen, H.C. and Ritter, J.R. (2000). The seven percent solution. *Journal of Finance*, 55(3), 1105–1132.

Clark, K. and Ofek, E. (1994). Mergers as a means of restructuring distressed firms: An empirical investigation. *Journal of Financial and Quantitative Analysis*, 29(4), 541–565.

Damodaran, A. (2009). Valuing young, start-up and growth companies: Estimation issues and valuation challenges. *SSRN*, June.

Dickinson, J.P. and Kyuno, K. (1977). Corporate valuation: A reconciliation of the Miller-Modigliani and traditionalist views. *Journal of Business Finance and Accounting*, 4(2), 177–185.

Duffie, D. and Singleton, K.J. (1999). Modeling terms structures of defaultable bonds. *The Review of Financial Studies*, 12(4), 687–720.

Eberhart, A., Altman, E., and Aggarwal, R. (1998). The equity performance of firms emerging from bankruptcy. *Journal of Finance*, 54(5), 1855–1868.

Ellert, J.C. (1976). Mergers, antitrust law enforcement and stockholder returns. *Journal of Finance*, 31(2), 715–732.

Ernst, Y. (2007). L'évaluation des actifs incorporels. Option Finance, H22, July.

Farrar, D.E. and Selwyn, L.L. (1967). Taxes, corporate financial policies and returns to investors. *National Tax Journal*, 20(4), 444–454.

Gillet, P. (2009). Les différents modes de financements et la structure optimale du capital. Course, Université Paris-Dauphine, Paris.

Gilson, S.C. (1995). Investing in distressed situations: A market survey. *Financial Analysts Journal*, 51(6), 8–27.

Gilson, S.C. (1997). Transactions costs and capital structure choice: Evidence from financially distressed firms. *Journal of Finance*, 52(1), 161–196.

Gilson, S.C., Hotchkiss, E.S., and Ruback, R.S. (2000). Valuation of bankrupt firms. *Review of Financial Studies*, 13(1), 43–74.

Gordon, M.J. and Shapiro, E. (1956). Capital equipment analysis: The required rate of profit. *Management Science*, 3(1), 102–110.

Graham, J.R. and Harvey, C.R. (2001). The theory and practice of corporate finance: Evidence from the field. *Journal of Financial Economics*, 60(2–3), 187–243.

Hamada, R.S. (1972). The effect of the firm's capital structure on the systematic risk of common stock. *Journal of Finance*, 27(2), 435–452.

Hambrick, D. and Hiller, N. (2005). Conceptualizing executive hubris: The role of (hyper)-core self-evaluations in strategic decision making. *Strategic Management Journal*, 26(4), 297–319.

Hansen, R. (1985). Auctions with contingent payments. *American Economic Review*, 75(4), 862–865.

Hansen, R. (2001). Do investment banks compete in IPOs? The advent of the seven percent plus contract. *Journal of Financial Economics*, 59(3), 313–346.

Heller, D. (2014). *Air France-KLM, structurer une analyse financière, 15 études de cas*. StudyramaPro, Levallois-Perret.

Heller, D. and Levyne, O. (2016). Cinema industry: Usefulness of the real options approach for valuation purpose. *International Journal of Business*, 21(1), 26–41.

Hotchkiss, E.S. (1995). Post-bankruptcy performance and management turnover. *Journal of Finance*, 50(1), 3–21.

Hotchkiss, E.S. and Mooradian, R.M. (1998). Acquisitions as a means of restructuring firms in Chapter 11. *Journal of Financial Intermediation*, 7(3), 240–262.

Ibboston, R.G., Sindelar, J.L., and Ritter, J.R. (1994). The market's problems with the pricing of initial public offerings. *Journal of Applied Corporate Finance*, 7(1), 66–74.

Jensen, M.C. (1989). Active investors, LBOs and the privatization of bankruptcy. *Journal of Applied Corporate Finance*, 2(1), 35–44.

Jensen, M.C., and Meckling, W. (1976). Theory of the firm: Managerial behavior, agency costs and ownership structure. *Journal of Financial Economics*, 3(4), 305–360.

John, K. (1987). Risk-shifting incentives and signalling through corporate structure. *Journal of Finance*, 42(3), 623–641.

Kaplan, S. (1989). Sources of value in management buyouts. In *Leveraged Management Buyout: Causes and Consequences*, Amihud, Y. (ed.). Dow Jones-Irwin, Homewood, 611–632.

Kaplan, S. and Ruback, R. (1995). The valuation of cash flow forecasts: An empirical analysis. *Journal of Finance*, 50(4), 1059–1093.

Kaplan, S. and Weisbach, R. (1992). The success of acquisitions: Evidence from divestitures. *Journal of Finance*, 47(1), 107–138.

Kim, M. and Ritter, J.R. (1999). Valuing IPOs. *Journal of Financial Economics*, 53(3), 409–437.

LeClair, M.S. (1990). Valuing the closely-held corporation: The validity and performance of established valuation procedures. *Accounting Horizons*, 3(4), 31–42.

Le Fur, Y. and Quiry, P. (2003). Besoin en fonds de roulement et endettement financier : où mettre la frontière ? *Vernimmen*, 18.

Le Fur, Y. and Quiry, P. (2004). Faut-il dans la valorisation des capitaux propres évaluer la dette en valeur de marché ? *Vernimmen*, 31.

Le Fur, Y. and Quiry, P. (2007). Faut-il, dans la méthode des comparables, calculer les multiples sur la base des valeurs actuelles de l'actif économique ou de valeurs prévisionnables ? *Vernimmen*, 55.

Le Fur, Y. and Quiry, P. (2010). Comment valoriser une entreprise qui a un immobilier d'exploitation important ? *Vernimmen*, 83.

Lewellen, W., Loderer, C., and Rosenfield, A. (1985). Merger decision and executive stock ownership in acquiring firms. *Journal of Accounting and Economics*, 7(1–3), 209–231.

Lie, E. and Lie, H.J. (2002). Multiples used to estimate corporate value. *Financial Analysts Journal*, 58(2), 44–54.

Lintner, J. (1965). The valuation of risk assets and the selection of risky investments in stock portfolios and capital budgets. *Review of Economics and Statistics*, 47(1), 13–37.

Litterman, R. and Iben, T. (1991). Corporate bond valuation and the term structure of credit spreads. *Journal of Portfolio Management*, 17(3), 52–64.

Litzenberger, R.H. and Rao, C.U. (1971). Estimates of the marginal rate of time preference and average risk aversion of investors in electric utility shares: 1960–1966. *The Bell Journal of Economics and Management Science*, 2(1), 265–277.

Liu, C. and Ziebart, D. (1994). Explaining earning quality – A market based test of a simple measure of sustainable earnings. Working document, University of Illinois, Urbana–Champaign.

Loughram, T. and Ritter, J. (2002). Why don't issuers get upset about leaving money on the table in IPOs? *Review of Financial Studies*, 15(2), 413–443.

Luehrman, T.A. (1997). Using APV: A better tool for valuing operations. *Harvard Business Review*, 145–154, May–June.

Macaulay, F. (1938). The movements of interest rates. Bond yields and stock prices in the United States since 1856. National Bureau of Economic Research, New York.

Mandelker, G. (1974). Risk and return: The case of merging firms. *Journal of Financial Economics*, 1(4).

Markowitz, H.M. (1959). *Portfolio Selection: Efficient Diversification of Investments*. Wiley, New York.

Masulis, R., Wang, C. and Xie, F. (2007). Corporate governance and acquirer returns. *Journal of Finance*, 62(4), 1851–1889.

Milicevic, B. (2009). The standard multiples valuation method and its criticism. *Economic Theme*, 47(4), 201–217.

Miller, M. (1977). Debt and taxes. *Journal of Finance*, 32(2), 261–276.

Modigliani, F. and Miller, M. (1958). The cost of capital, corporation finance and the theory of investment. *The American Economic Review*, 48(3), 261–297.

Modigliani, F. and Miller, M. (1963). Corporate income taxes and the cost of capital: A correction. *The American Economic Review*, 53(3), 433–443.

Moeller, S., Schlingemann, F., and Stulz, R. (2004). Firm size and the gains from acquisitions. *Journal of Financial Economics*, 73(2), 201–228.

Moeller, S., Schlingemann, F., and Stulz, R. (2005). Wealth destruction on a massive scale? A study of acquiring-firm returns in the recent merger wave. *Journal of Finance*, 60(2), 757–82.

Molina, C. (2005). Are firms underleveraged? An examination of the effect of leverage on defaults probabilities. *Journal of Finance*, 60(3), 1427–1459.

Mossin, J. (1966). Equilibrium in a capital asset market. *Econometrica*, 34(4), 768–783.

Myers, S.C. (1974). Interactions of corporate financing and investment decisions – Implications for capital budgeting. *The Journal of Finance*, 29(1), 1–23.

Myers, S.C. and Majluf, N.S. (1984). Corporate financing and investment decisions when firms have information that investors do not have. *Journal of Financial Economics*, 13(2), 187–221.

Narayanan, M. (1988). Debt versus equity under asymmetric information. *Journal of Financial and Quantitative Analysis*, 23(1), 39–51.

Ofek, E. (1993). Capital structure and firm response to poor performance: An empirical investigation. *Journal of Financial Economics*, 34(1), 3–30.

Ohlson, J.A. (1995). Earnings, book values and dividends in equity valuation. *Contemporary Accounting Research*, 11(2), 661–687.

Pecherot, B. (2000). Les acquisitions par offres publiques : création de valeur et stratégie des acquéreurs. PhD Thesis, Université Grenoble II, Saint-Martin-d'Hères.

Pye, G. (1974). Gauging the default premium. *Financial Analysts Journal*, 30(1), 49–50.

Roll, R. (1986). The hubris hypothesis of corporate takeovers. *Journal of Business*, 59(2), 197–216.

Ross, S. (1977). The determination of financial structure: The incentive-signalling approach. *Bell Journal of Economics*, 8(1), 23–40.

Ruback, R. (1986). Calculating the market value of riskless cash flows. *Journal of Financial Economics*, 15(13), 323–339.

Ruback, R. (1998). Capital cash flows: A simple approach to valuing risky cash flows. Working paper, Harvard Business School, Boston.

Scarberry, M., Klee, K., Newton, G., and Nickles, S. (1996). *Business Reorganization in Bankruptcy: Cases and Materials*. West Publishing Co., St Paul.

Shaffer, S. (2006). Corporate failure and equity valuation. *Financial Analysts Journal*, 62(1), 71–80.

Sharpe, W.F. (1963). A simplified model for portfolio analysis. *Management Science*, 9(1), 277–293.

Sharpe, W.F. (1964). Capital asset prices: A theory of market equilibrium under conditions of risk. *Journal of Finance*, 19(3), 425–442.

Shleifer, A. and Vishny, R. (1986). Greenmail white knights and shareholder's interest. *Rand Journal of Economics*, 17(3), 293–309.

Shleifer, A. and Vishny, R. (1997). A survey of corporate governance. *The Journal of Finance*, 52(2), 737–783.

Smith, A.J. (1990). Capital ownership structure and performance: The case of management buyouts. *Journal of Financial Economics*, 27(1), 143–164.

Smith, C.W. and Warner, J.B. (1979). On financial contracting. *Journal of Financial Economics*, 7(2), 117–161.

Thauvron, A. (2009). *Évaluation d'entreprise*. Economica, Paris.

Tietmann, J. (1986). *Applications of Auction Games in Mergers and Acquisitions: The White Knight Takeover Defense*. Harvard Business School, Boston.

Tinic, S.M. and West, R.R. (1984). Risk and return: January vs. The rest of the year. *Journal of Financial Economics*, 13(4), 564–574.

Varaiya, N., Bergmar, B., and Taylor, R. (1997). F&C International: A case study of an IPO valuation. *Journal of Financial Education*, 23, 114–123.

Vernimmen, P. (2012). *Finance d'entreprise*. Dalloz, Paris.

Watson, J. and Everett, J. (1996). Do small businesses have high failure rates? *Journal of Small Business Manangement*, 34(4), 45–63.

Welch, I. (1989). Seasoned offerings, imitation costs and the underpricing of initial public offerings. *Journal of Finance*, 44(2), 421–449.

Zarowin, P. (1990). What determines earnings-price ratios: Revisited. *Journal of Accounting Audit & Finance*, 5, 439–454.

Index

R, S, T

Other titles from

iSTE

in

Innovation, Entrepreneurship and Management

2021

BOBILLIER CHAUMON Marc-Eric
Digital Transformations in the Challenge of Activity and Work: Understanding and Supporting Technological Changes
(Technological Changes and Human Resources Set – Volume 3)

2020

ACH Yves-Alain, RMADI-SAÏD Sandra
Financial Information and Brand Value: Reflections, Challenges and Limitations

ANDREOSSO-O'CALLAGHAN Bernadette, DZEVER Sam, JAUSSAUD Jacques, TAYLOR Robert
Sustainable Development and Energy Transition in Europe and Asia
(Innovation and Technology Set – Volume 9)

BEN SLIMANE Sonia, M'HENNI Hatem
Entrepreneurship and Development: Realities and Future Prospects
(Smart Innovation Set – Volume 30)

CHOUTEAU Marianne, FOREST Joëlle, NGUYEN Céline
Innovation for Society: The P.S.I. Approach
(Smart Innovation Set – Volume 28)

CORON Clotilde
Quantifying Human Resources: Uses and Analysis
(Technological Changes and Human Resources Set – Volume 2)

CORON Clotilde, GILBERT Patrick
Technological Change
(Technological Changes and Human Resources Set – Volume 1)

CERDIN Jean-Luc, PERETTI Jean-Marie
The Success of Apprenticeships: Views of Stakeholders on Training and Learning
(Human Resources Management Set – Volume 3)

DELCHET-COCHET Karen
Circular Economy: From Waste Reduction to Value Creation
(Economic Growth Set – Volume 2)

DIDAY Edwin, GUAN Rong, SAPORTA Gilbert, WANG Huiwen
Advances in Data Science
(Big Data, Artificial Intelligence and Data Analysis Set – Volume 4)

DOS SANTOS PAULINO Victor
Innovation Trends in the Space Industry
(Smart Innovation Set – Volume 25)

GASMI Nacer
Corporate Innovation Strategies: Corporate Social Responsibility and Shared Value Creation
(Smart Innovation Set – Volume 33)

GOGLIN Christian
Emotions and Values in Equity Crowdfunding Investment Choices 1: Transdisciplinary Theoretical Approach

GUILHON Bernard
Venture Capital and the Financing of Innovation
(Innovation Between Risk and Reward Set – Volume 6)

LATOUCHE Pascal
Open Innovation: Human Set-up
(Innovation and Technology Set – Volume 10)

LIMA Marcos
Entrepreneurship and Innovation Education: Frameworks and Tools
(Smart Innovation Set – Volume 32)

MACHADO Carolina, DAVIM J. Paulo
Sustainable Management for Managers and Engineers

MAKRIDES Andreas, KARAGRIGORIOU Alex, SKIADAS Christos H.
Data Analysis and Applications 3: Computational, Classification, Financial, Statistical and Stochastic Methods
(Big Data, Artificial Intelligence and Data Analysis Set – Volume 5)
Data Analysis and Applications 4: Financial Data Analysis and Methods
(Big Data, Artificial Intelligence and Data Analysis Set – Volume 6)

MASSOTTE Pierre, CORSI Patrick
Complex Decision-Making in Economy and Finance

MEUNIER François-Xavier
Dual Innovation Systems: Concepts, Tools and Methods
(Smart Innovation Set – Volume 31)

MICHAUD Thomas
Science Fiction and Innovation Design (Innovation in Engineering and Technology Set – Volume 6)

MONINO Jean-Louis
Data Control: Major Challenge for the Digital Society
(Smart Innovation Set – Volume 29)

MORLAT Clément
Sustainable Productive System: Eco-development versus Sustainable Development
(Smart Innovation Set – Volume 26)

SAULAIS Pierre, ERMINE Jean-Louis
Knowledge Management in Innovative Companies 2: Understanding and Deploying a KM Plan within a Learning Organization
(Smart Innovation Set – Volume 27)

2019

AMENDOLA Mario, GAFFARD Jean-Luc
Disorder and Public Concern Around Globalization

BARBAROUX Pierre
Disruptive Technology and Defence Innovation Ecosystems
(Innovation in Engineering and Technology Set – Volume 5)

DOU Henri, JUILLET Alain, CLERC Philippe
Strategic Intelligence for the Future 1: A New Strategic and Operational Approach
Strategic Intelligence for the Future 2: A New Information Function Approach

FRIKHA Azza
Measurement in Marketing: Operationalization of Latent Constructs

FRIMOUSSE Soufyane
Innovation and Agility in the Digital Age
(Human Resources Management Set – Volume 2)

GAY Claudine, SZOSTAK Bérangère L.
Innovation and Creativity in SMEs: Challenges, Evolutions and Prospects
(Smart Innovation Set – Volume 21)

GORIA Stéphane, HUMBERT Pierre, ROUSSEL Benoît
Information, Knowledge and Agile Creativity
(Smart Innovation Set – Volume 22)

HELLER David
Investment Decision-making Using Optional Models
(Economic Growth Set – Volume 2)

HELLER David, DE CHADIRAC Sylvain, HALAOUI Lana, JOUVET Camille
The Emergence of Start-ups
(Economic Growth Set – Volume 1)

HÉRAUD Jean-Alain, KERR Fiona, BURGER-HELMCHEN Thierry
Creative Management of Complex Systems
(Smart Innovation Set – Volume 19)

LATOUCHE Pascal
Open Innovation: Corporate Incubator
(Innovation and Technology Set – Volume 7)

LEHMANN Paul-Jacques
The Future of the Euro Currency

LEIGNEL Jean-Louis, MENAGER Emmanuel, YABLONSKY Serge
Sustainable Enterprise Performance: A Comprehensive Evaluation Method

LIÈVRE Pascal, AUBRY Monique, GAREL Gilles
Management of Extreme Situations: From Polar Expeditions to Exploration-Oriented Organizations

MILLOT Michel
Embarrassment of Product Choices 2: Towards a Society of Well-being

N'GOALA Gilles, PEZ-PÉRARD Virginie, PRIM-ALLAZ Isabelle
Augmented Customer Strategy: CRM in the Digital Age

NIKOLOVA Blagovesta
The RRI Challenge: Responsibilization in a State of Tension with Market Regulation
(Innovation and Responsibility Set – Volume 3)

PELLEGRIN-BOUCHER Estelle, ROY Pierre
Innovation in the Cultural and Creative Industries
(Innovation and Technology Set – Volume 8)

PRIOLON Joël
Financial Markets for Commodities

QUINIOU Matthieu
Blockchain: The Advent of Disintermediation

RAVIX Joël-Thomas, DESCHAMPS Marc
Innovation and Industrial Policies
(Innovation between Risk and Reward Set – Volume 5)

ROGER Alain, VINOT Didier
Skills Management: New Applications, New Questions
(Human Resources Management Set – Volume 1)

SAULAIS Pierre, ERMINE Jean-Louis
Knowledge Management in Innovative Companies 1: Understanding and Deploying a KM Plan within a Learning Organization
(Smart Innovation Set – Volume 23)

SERVAJEAN-HILST Romaric
Co-innovation Dynamics: The Management of Client-Supplier Interactions for Open Innovation
(Smart Innovation Set – Volume 20)

SKIADAS Christos H., BOZEMAN James R.
Data Analysis and Applications 1: Clustering and Regression, Modeling-estimating, Forecasting and Data Mining
(Big Data, Artificial Intelligence and Data Analysis Set – Volume 2)
Data Analysis and Applications 2: Utilization of Results in Europe and Other Topics
(Big Data, Artificial Intelligence and Data Analysis Set – Volume 3)

UZUNIDIS Dimitri
Systemic Innovation: Entrepreneurial Strategies and Market Dynamics

VIGEZZI Michel
World Industrialization: Shared Inventions, Competitive Innovations and Social Dynamics
(Smart Innovation Set – Volume 24)

2018

BURKHARDT Kirsten
Private Equity Firms: Their Role in the Formation of Strategic Alliances

CALLENS Stéphane
Creative Globalization
(Smart Innovation Set – Volume 16)

CASADELLA Vanessa
Innovation Systems in Emerging Economies: MINT – Mexico, Indonesia, Nigeria, Turkey
(Smart Innovation Set – Volume 18)

CHOUTEAU Marianne, FOREST Joëlle, NGUYEN Céline
Science, Technology and Innovation Culture
(Innovation in Engineering and Technology Set – Volume 3)

CORLOSQUET-HABART Marine, JANSSEN Jacques
Big Data for Insurance Companies
(Big Data, Artificial Intelligence and Data Analysis Set – Volume 1)

CROS Françoise
Innovation and Society
(Smart Innovation Set – Volume 15)

DEBREF Romain
Environmental Innovation and Ecodesign: Certainties and Controversies
(Smart Innovation Set – Volume 17)

DOMINGUEZ Noémie
SME Internationalization Strategies: Innovation to Conquer New Markets

ERMINE Jean-Louis
Knowledge Management: The Creative Loop
(Innovation and Technology Set – Volume 5)

GILBERT Patrick, BOBADILLA Natalia, GASTALDI Lise,
LE BOULAIRE Martine, LELEBINA Olga
Innovation, Research and Development Management

IBRAHIMI Mohammed
Mergers & Acquisitions: Theory, Strategy, Finance

LEMAÎTRE Denis
Training Engineers for Innovation

LÉVY Aldo, BEN BOUHENI Faten, AMMI Chantal
Financial Management: USGAAP and IFRS Standards
(Innovation and Technology Set – Volume 6)

MILLOT Michel
Embarrassment of Product Choices 1: How to Consume Differently

PANSERA Mario, OWEN Richard
Innovation and Development: The Politics at the Bottom of the Pyramid
(Innovation and Responsibility Set – Volume 2)

RICHEZ Yves
Corporate Talent Detection and Development

SACHETTI Philippe, ZUPPINGER Thibaud
New Technologies and Branding
(Innovation and Technology Set – Volume 4)

SAMIER Henri
Intuition, Creativity, Innovation

TEMPLE Ludovic, COMPAORÉ SAWADOGO Eveline M.F.W.
Innovation Processes in Agro-Ecological Transitions in Developing Countries
(Innovation in Engineering and Technology Set – Volume 2)

UZUNIDIS Dimitri
Collective Innovation Processes: Principles and Practices
(Innovation in Engineering and Technology Set – Volume 4)

VAN HOOREBEKE Delphine
The Management of Living Beings or Emo-management

2017

AÏT-EL-HADJ Smaïl
The Ongoing Technological System
(Smart Innovation Set – Volume 11)

BAUDRY Marc, DUMONT Béatrice
Patents: Prompting or Restricting Innovation?
(Smart Innovation Set – Volume 12)

BÉRARD Céline, TEYSSIER Christine
Risk Management: Lever for SME Development and Stakeholder Value Creation

CHALENÇON Ludivine
Location Strategies and Value Creation of International Mergers and Acquisitions

CHAUVEL Danièle, BORZILLO Stefano
The Innovative Company: An Ill-defined Object
(Innovation between Risk and Reward Set – Volume 1)

CORSI Patrick
Going Past Limits To Growth

D'ANDRIA Aude, GABARRET Inés
Building 21st Century Entrepreneurship
(Innovation and Technology Set – Volume 2)

DAIDJ Nabyla
Cooperation, Coopetition and Innovation
(Innovation and Technology Set – Volume 3)

FERNEZ-WALCH Sandrine
The Multiple Facets of Innovation Project Management
(Innovation between Risk and Reward Set – Volume 4)

FOREST Joëlle
Creative Rationality and Innovation
(Smart Innovation Set – Volume 14)

GUILHON Bernard
Innovation and Production Ecosystems
(Innovation between Risk and Reward Set – Volume 2)

HAMMOUDI Abdelhakim, DAIDJ Nabyla
Game Theory Approach to Managerial Strategies and Value Creation
(Diverse and Global Perspectives on Value Creation Set – Volume 3)

LALLEMENT Rémi
Intellectual Property and Innovation Protection: New Practices and New Policy Issues
(Innovation between Risk and Reward Set – Volume 3)

LAPERCHE Blandine
Enterprise Knowledge Capital
(Smart Innovation Set – Volume 13)

LEBERT Didier, EL YOUNSI Hafida
International Specialization Dynamics
(Smart Innovation Set – Volume 9)

MAESSCHALCK Marc
Reflexive Governance for Research and Innovative Knowledge
(Responsible Research and Innovation Set – Volume 6)

MASSOTTE Pierre
Ethics in Social Networking and Business 1: Theory, Practice and Current Recommendations
Ethics in Social Networking and Business 2: The Future and Changing Paradigms

MASSOTTE Pierre, CORSI Patrick
Smart Decisions in Complex Systems

MEDINA Mercedes, HERRERO Mónica, URGELLÉS Alicia
Current and Emerging Issues in the Audiovisual Industry
(Diverse and Global Perspectives on Value Creation Set – Volume 1)

MICHAUD Thomas
Innovation, Between Science and Science Fiction
(Smart Innovation Set – Volume 10)

PELLÉ Sophie
Business, Innovation and Responsibility
(Responsible Research and Innovation Set – Volume 7)

SAVIGNAC Emmanuelle
The Gamification of Work: The Use of Games in the Workplace

SUGAHARA Satoshi, DAIDJ Nabyla, USHIO Sumitaka
Value Creation in Management Accounting and Strategic Management: An Integrated Approach
(Diverse and Global Perspectives on Value Creation Set –Volume 2)

UZUNIDIS Dimitri, SAULAIS Pierre
Innovation Engines: Entrepreneurs and Enterprises in a Turbulent World
(Innovation in Engineering and Technology Set – Volume 1)

2016

BARBAROUX Pierre, ATTOUR Amel, SCHENK Eric
Knowledge Management and Innovation
(Smart Innovation Set – Volume 6)

BEN BOUHENI Faten, AMMI Chantal, LEVY Aldo
Banking Governance, Performance And Risk-Taking: Conventional Banks Vs Islamic Banks

BOUTILLIER Sophie, CARRÉ Denis, LEVRATTO Nadine
Entrepreneurial Ecosystems (Smart Innovation Set – Volume 2)

BOUTILLIER Sophie, UZUNIDIS Dimitri
The Entrepreneur (Smart Innovation Set – Volume 8)

BOUVARD Patricia, SUZANNE Hervé
Collective Intelligence Development in Business

GALLAUD Delphine, LAPERCHE Blandine
Circular Economy, Industrial Ecology and Short Supply Chains
(Smart Innovation Set – Volume 4)

GUERRIER Claudine
Security and Privacy in the Digital Era
(Innovation and Technology Set – Volume 1)

MEGHOUAR Hicham
Corporate Takeover Targets

MONINO Jean-Louis, SEDKAOUI Soraya
Big Data, Open Data and Data Development
(Smart Innovation Set – Volume 3)

MOREL Laure, LE ROUX Serge
Fab Labs: Innovative User
(Smart Innovation Set – Volume 5)

PICARD Fabienne, TANGUY Corinne
Innovations and Techno-ecological Transition
(Smart Innovation Set – Volume 7)

2015

CASADELLA Vanessa, LIU Zeting, DIMITRI Uzunidis
Innovation Capabilities and Economic Development in Open Economies
(Smart Innovation Set – Volume 1)

CORSI Patrick, MORIN Dominique
Sequencing Apple's DNA

CORSI Patrick, NEAU Erwan
Innovation Capability Maturity Model

FAIVRE-TAVIGNOT Bénédicte
Social Business and Base of the Pyramid

GODÉ Cécile
Team Coordination in Extreme Environments

MAILLARD Pierre
Competitive Quality and Innovation

MASSOTTE Pierre, CORSI Patrick
Operationalizing Sustainability

MASSOTTE Pierre, CORSI Patrick
Sustainability Calling

2014

DUBÉ Jean, LEGROS Diègo
Spatial Econometrics Using Microdata

LESCA Humbert, LESCA Nicolas
Strategic Decisions and Weak Signals

2013

HABART-CORLOSQUET Marine, JANSSEN Jacques, MANCA Raimondo
VaR Methodology for Non-Gaussian Finance

2012

DAL PONT Jean-Pierre
Process Engineering and Industrial Management

MAILLARD Pierre
Competitive Quality Strategies

POMEROL Jean-Charles
Decision-Making and Action

SZYLAR Christian
UCITS Handbook

2011

LESCA Nicolas
Environmental Scanning and Sustainable Development

LESCA Nicolas, LESCA Humbert
Weak Signals for Strategic Intelligence: Anticipation Tool for Managers

MERCIER-LAURENT Eunika
Innovation Ecosystems

2010

SZYLAR Christian
Risk Management under UCITS III/IV

2009

COHEN Corine
Business Intelligence

ZANINETTI Jean-Marc
Sustainable Development in the USA

2008

CORSI Patrick, DULIEU Mike
The Marketing of Technology Intensive Products and Services

DZEVER Sam, JAUSSAUD Jacques, ANDREOSSO Bernadette
Evolving Corporate Structures and Cultures in Asia: Impact of Globalization

2007

AMMI Chantal
Global Consumer Behavior

2006

BOUGHZALA Imed, ERMINE Jean-Louis
Trends in Enterprise Knowledge Management

CORSI Patrick *et al.*
Innovation Engineering: the Power of Intangible Networks

CPSIA information can be obtained
at www.ICGtesting.com
Printed in the USA
JSHW041205250421
13931JS00001B/4

9 781786 306364